GROWING UP IN THE WEST

by

Phillip E Payne

authorHOUSE®

AuthorHouse™
1663 Liberty Drive, Suite 200
Bloomington, IN 47403
www.authorhouse.com
Phone: 1-800-839-8640

First published by AuthorHouse 10/2/2007

ISBN: 978-1-4343-2183-1 (sc)
ISBN: 978-1-4343-2182-4 (hc)

Printed in the United States of America
Bloomington, Indiana

This book is printed on acid-free paper.

CHAPTER 1
EARLIEST MEMORIES

Warm, cozy, mother humming a song, are the earliest of my memories. Mother was always there. As I began school, I discovered that many Fathers, unlike mine, rarely were away from home. My Father, Dad, Bill (William) Markanis, was away most of the time working on a road bed, bridge or engines, but always on the railroads. My name is Luke.

Mother (Jane) catered to my every need, and taught me those things all young boy children must acquire. Perhaps my best memory was the knowledge that I had a good, secure, safe home to go to at the end of the day. She was a good cook too. We often had neighbors during my early years, and we, like so many children, were deeply involved in playing cowboys and Indians. When we were at a lonesome place, where only adults worked, Mother often read to me. She taught me to appreciate good books. She could even make the stories from the Bible exciting. On occasion, we were able to see what we called Wild Indians. However, mother did not want me fraternizing with Indians.

Normally, I could say that I was an obedient son, but Indians were the topic of conversations, both at the dining table and in the parlor. Contrary to what mothers think, her limiting my contact with Indians, made me want to know even more about them. When I was about seven, I made friends with an Indian boy my age.

His name was Little Crow, named for an Eastern Sioux Chief of the Dakota Tribe. I had a great admiration for Little Crow, because they lived in a Teepee, and like us, they moved around a lot. Contrary to what I thought, there was a lot of room inside a Teepee. Yes, it was cozy, but warm in the winter. To be honest, I probably fancied their life; where their type of schooling was taught while they lived on the plains wilderness. The subjects taught, could almost immediately, be put into practice. Little Crow was a walking library of plants, tracks of animals and edible roots. Once, he showed me a plant that when wetted and placed on a wound, would help it to heal.

I knew that many people did not like to see the Indians around; they seemed to be afraid that they would go on the War Path. From my contact with Little Crow, I knew they were just trying to feed their families. I made it a point to sneak a bit of food for Little Crow every time I visited them. I suppose that I knew there was bad Indians, just like the White Man's outlaws, however I knew that Little Crow and his family only wanted to survive.

Like many an innocent child, when playing with Little Crow, I thought that I was getting away with something big, but later I discovered that my Father knew all about our friendship. One of the best times was when my Father and I rode with Little Crow and his Father on a hunt. We had great fun hunting pheasants, quail, and another upland fowl. We all laughed when Little Crow's Father shot his ancient muzzle-loading shotgun. It had a tendency to come apart when fired. Then one day, father loaded all of our things in a wagon, and we traveled for several days west to a bridge site on the Union Pacific Railroad.

We spent several days in that wagon; riding behind six mules. Often I would jump down to investigate an animal or just an animal's hole in the ground. This was in the tall grass country, and it seemed never to stop waving in the wind. "Like waves on the ocean," my father said. Often we would see herds of Buffalo; Big Buffalos; especially the bulls. The calves were often curious, and would stand and watch us passing by, until their mothers growled, then they would run to her. Once my father said, "One day all of this will be planted in wheat, enough can be grown here to feed the world." At the time I thought he was stretching that some, but it proved true.

Once, I asked my Father why Little Crow and his sister Bright Star did not attend the school. He took some time to think about that question. When the answer came, his answer was not what I expected. He did explain the history of the Indian wars, and why many whites feared the Indians to the point that they wished that, all Indians were dead. All of which was a bit confusing, because my best friend was an Indian.

I was proud of my Father. He had some special talent in constructing bridges and railroad roadbeds. He worked for several railroads. One summer in Missouri, he supervised cutting trees down for railroad ties. I watched from our wagon, as the trees all over the side of a mountain were cut down. Then, made into railroad ties, and shipped to the railhead. Men that worked building the railroads were hearty, strong, and worked long hours. Many were from Ireland, and had recently immigrated to America. Others included men from China. It was on a work site in the west that I saw my first Chinaman.

Generally, the Chinese workers were thin, but worked well together, and ate a lot of rice (Ugh). They often wore a long 'night-gown' thing, which blew in the wind. Straw hats were their normal head cover, and it was interesting to see how they worked together to lift and place the ties and rails. I did not like it when my Father was working at the railhead, it was dusty, cold, or hot, and the food was mostly Buffalo and Elk steaks. Well, the hump meat of the Buffalo was not bad. The drive to build railroads in the west was intense, and to keep construction on schedule, many near inhuman things were seen. I did not like to think about that.

Accidents often happened, legs, arms and fingers and feet were sometime crushed, then had to be cut off. There was little sympathy on the railroad's part, and an injured worker had to heal himself, then, go back to work; if he could. Dust and dirt were more than plentiful. Body washing was a rare thing. Of course, my mother never let a Saturday pass but I had to have a bath. I was often embarrassed when she would stand me in a creek and scrub me down. The workers watched and laughed.

The best times were when father built a Depot in a town, switching yards, or other sidetracks. Always there were children to play with, and have foot races and such. Many families lived close to the earth; a term my Father often used to describe them. Naturally, I preferred living in a town, even better we often lived in a hotel or rooming house. That was neat!

Those are the times, when I had the opportunity to attend school. Mostly I just listened, and did the homework. Mother saw to that every day. These school teachers, usually only one to a school, knew I was not going to be there very long, and my parents would probably not even come to discuss my progress, or lack there of. I knew my mother would see the teacher, because she somehow obtained textbooks, and taught me from them when there was no school nearby. My mother was able to teach in a way, that it did not seem to be drudgery. When I once complained of a writing assignment, she said, "Luke, where would we be if the writers of the Bible had not learned to write." Probably, the most memorable time was when I attended a Mormon school.

I liked the students. They were easy to get to know, but always called me, "One of those Infidels." However, they played games fairly, and rarely caused arguments. Some of them could read most anything, and once a fellow my age quoted nearly a complete page from the Bible. Anyway, they were nice and always eager to swap things at lunch. One thing that I did not like was their constant invitation for me to 'get baptized'. Once they invited me to go to a baptism for two eight-year-old girls. Now, I do not want to get you thinking wrong, but there was a special feeling at that baptism service. Someone had said, "The spirit was really strong at that service." I suppose that is what I was feeling; but it soon passed.

Like every other boy, my great desire was to have a horse of my own. However, my Father was dead-set against it. Nevertheless, I had frequent opportunities to ride and even drive a team. At every school I attended, several of the students rode a horse to school, and hobbled them nearby. This led to invitations, to let me ride with them, to our home on the way to their home, and some horse racing. Most of the boys from Ranches carried pistols or rifles when going to or from the school. When I suggested to father that I too needed a pistol, he said, "I think not."

When I was almost nine years old, my mother got sick, and we had to have someone to help in the home. For a while mother had to be near a good doctor, and we lived in a suburb of Kansas City. Those housekeepers were sometime strong and sometime careless. I tried to discover their special fussy things, the things they thought were very important, and if I obeyed those, normally I would have a free reign. Kansas City was an interesting place. Lots of people, tall buildings, and many pioneers were traveling west. I wanted to go west and see the

Buffalo and the mountains, but I knew better than try anything foolish.

After several months in the big city, they called my Father home, because they could not make mother well. Those dumb doctors! It was a sad time, a time about which I do not like to think. After the funeral, many urged my Father to place me in a home or orphanage. I was afraid that we may not be together; many suggested that I would be better off in a home. He would have none of it.

He made me a kit, containing clothes and personal items. He bought me some good warm clothes, and I traveled with him on his jobs, and went to the local schools, when possible. At first, this new life style was exciting, riding trains and horses and being with my Father every day; I was able to see many things and ride often on work trains.

Work trains are a special train that often had dormitories and cooking facilities. Most were equipped with a steam-powered wench and lifting jig, used to replace and raise other heavy items. It was on one of these special trains that I heard my father ask a worker to, "Not use that fowl language in front of my son." Now, I had heard it all, and said so to Father, but he said, "If one hears that cursing over and over, it will become a natural part of your vocabulary." I noticed a change in the workers speaking after that. This event made me realize that my Father was different. Although, he often worked right along side the laborers, he was recognized as different; a step above the normal. I do not mean that he was 'uppity', but he paid close attention to his clothes and personal hygiene.

As the railroad engines were the monster machines of the day, I had a great desire to know how they worked. Engineers and Firemen were quick to answer my questions, and often would take time to tell a story of a success or failure. I was always a bit amazed at the depth of my Fathers knowledge of these steam engines. Being manufactured by several companies, and at a high rate, most conversations were about "The Next Big Locomotive."

Technologies were rapidly being developed that allowed these newer Locomotives to pull higher and higher loads. There was one invention that, although simple, made these engines more powerful. By having the steam coming out of the driving piston cylinder, go into another but smaller driving piston, resulted in additional power.

Like many things, the new traveling from job to job wore off, and it soon became a bit of drudgery. However, I was with my Father, and he did many things to try to keep me entertained. We traveled almost the whole of the western United States. "Riding the Rails," a popular used term in the 1870s, brought many encounters with Salesmen (Drummers), Cowboys, Buffalo hunters, and Immigrants.

Chapter 2
Traveling the Plains

I noted the wide variety of rich and poor, who came from Europe, but even the poor had shining eyes of hope to own their own land. Father said,

"These families know how to work, will raise good families, and will help our nation grow." The sounds of their foreign languages, and special dress styles, were always interesting. Costumes, is what Father called the immigrant's clothes. He said,

"Each country, and often even a section of a country, has their own costume and folk dances. The Royal Families, and aristocrats own most of Europe's land, and the immigrants we see are those who have escaped from a lifetime of oppression."

Riding on trains in the early 1870s, I marveled at the number of languages one encountered. I noted that most of the Immigrants seemed to look to the horizon, and were eagerly anticipating a new way of life. Some of their children were pale and sickly, but Father said that they would recover quickly when they get settled and have some proper food. Smells, I really was fascinated by the aroma of their sack/basket lunches'. They made my mouth water and me hungry. Getting anything good to eat on a train was difficult.

In 1872, when I was ten, and we were on our way to Denver, Colorado, much of the conversation in the passenger cars was about Colorado becoming a State, and Buffalo hunting. One day I sat next to some cowboys in their high-heeled boots, leather chaps, ten-gallon hats, pistols, and large jingling spurs. Almost all carried a saddle and rifle on-board the train with them. One was a remarkable site; his' hat seemed to fill the car when he stood-up. He said that his handle was "Tex." My Father had to explain that a 'handle' was a cowboy's name; or more likely his 'Nick Name'.

Most cowboys had salt stains on their shirts, and slick pants bottoms. When I pointed this out to Father, he said,

"They work from a saddle. Most days they will wear out two to three horses each day, herding cattle and horses." Some cowboys wore clothes that were old, and ragged, and should have been discarded long ago. You knew they were old because many were the ruminants of the Civil War uniforms.

I listened to that cowboy talk about a new Buffalo Bill Cody Wild West Show. I knew this name, because just recently the newspapers had stories about him. He was awarded the Congressional Medal of Honor, for being a top notch Army Scout. My Father asked many questions about this new show. Locals, who worked cattle every day, did not see much chance of it being successful. However, when they told of their plans to tour the eastern states, and perform stagecoach robberies, and fights with real Indians, my Father really thought it might be a moneymaker.

I lost interest when they began to talk about horses, cows and Buffalos for the show, but perked up when they described how they would reenact stagecoach hold-ups, and battles with Indians. My Father reminded me that these fellows had actually fought against some of the Indian Tribes, and the newspapers were still full of General Custer and his encounters with the Sioux.

At the next water station, my Father sent a telegram to the Denver & Rio Grande Railroad office, suggesting that someone contact an eastern railroad about providing transportation for the Buffalo Bill Cody Wild West Show. He thought that a special train would be required to transport all of the stock.

He was always doing things like that, and once I heard a railroad big shot (executive), give him a lot of credit for his foresight. Actually, he offered my Father a job, just traveling around and searching for opportunities for the railroads. Nevertheless, my Father liked 'hands-on' work, and was a kind of a troubleshooter for several railroads. In addition, he liked doing many jobs, he said,

"I learn a little here and there; always seeing what will and won't work."

Railroaders sure like to tell stories about their experiences. Once an engineer who was deadheading (traveling from his home to the point where he would become the engineer) stopped by when he saw my Father. It seemed like all railroad people knew my Father. They related an event that caught my attention. The first ever rail engine that came across Iowa (early 1800s), had to cross the Missouri River near Omaha. However, there was no bridge, and, the engine was to be floated across on a barge, and it was in the coldest part of the winter.

Missouri River banks are rather steep in that area, so a piece of track was constructed on the east side, down the bank to get the engine down to the barge. Being very heavy, on the way down the engine came lose, and quickly came down the track, crossed the barge, and went into the river. Only a few inches of the engine remained above the water.

A temporary lift system had to be fabricated to raise the engine, out of the water and onto the barge. By then the river was frozen-over, and axes had to be used to chop a clear path for the barge. On the west side of the

11

river, additional track was laid up the bank, and many volunteers and horses and mules from the local towns, came to help pull the engine up the bank. A simple river crossing had almost caused the loss of a steam engine.

Thus, the engine had crossed the Missouri River; however, there was no roadbed or tracks west of Omaha, and the engine just sat there until spring. My Father and the engineer, 'hee-hawed' repeatedly at the dumb mistakes that were made in getting that engine to the Nebraska side of the river.

It was listening to this tale, when I discovered that railroad engines, were described by its' number of wheels. An engine with a four-wheel front truck, a single driving wheel, and a four-wheel bogy on the back, was known as a 4-2-4. I even tried my hand at drawing a few of the engines. Later, I discovered that several companies built railroad steam engines, with each of the builders using their own design. Even to me it was apparent that every new engine design was bigger, more powerful, and faster.

Traveling across Kansas and Nebraska was often just flat boring. Flat land and rolling hills did not excite the eye.

Often it appeared like endless grassy plains. Then the train would come around a bend, and one could see for miles down a valley or streambed. Few trees were out there, and where water was near the surface, large Cottonwood Trees grew. Most of the settlements used the water to found their town. These plains were cold in the winter and hot in the summer, and the wind often blew.

In places, the sand hills were covered in long-stemmed grasses. There, one could not see very far, but the wind caused the grass to wave, providing a motion that many claimed looked very much like waves on the ocean. I have never seen an ocean.

In some places, usually farther west, the grass was much shorter, and provided a more varied scenic view. Alone, people often got lost, and afraid. Afraid because there was no one that could tell them what to do or where to go. People from the east, who had lived all of their life next to a neighbor, found the loneliness of the prairies to be unbearable, and often returned to 'civilization' in the east. To survive, one had to be able to navigate by the stars.

By seeking the Big Dipper, one can easily determine the direction of north. Some even took or made a simple level and string system, which roughly measured the Latitude. Very much like the navigators on ships on the oceans, these measurements were helpful in a gross sense. Nevertheless, it was a form of guidance. With the coming of the railroads, the tracks quickly were called the iron compass. It was common to hear a homesteader say, "My place is 'so many miles, north, or south of the railroad.' Even railroads had to prepare for these long, lonesome stretches of blowing grasses.

Because a railroad engine requires a lot of water with which to make steam, at frequent intervals along the railroad, water tanks were constructed. Usually supported with a windmill, these tanks would often be the first thing one could see before the next train stop. Once or twice father knew the engineer, and allowed me to ride in the engine. Noisy and busy, best describes the railroad engine. Firemen, feeding the engines, were constantly shoveling coal into the hopper, and metering water into the boiler. If asked to paint a picture of the average railroad man, I would draw a Conductor, looking at his pocket watch. Being on time was a must.

With trains traveling in both directions, one had to get onto a siding, to allow the oncoming train to pass. Often we would be sitting on a siding, and the passing train would pass so close that it looked like you could reach out at touch it. Once, father gave me his watch and had me write down the times we passed water tanks, towns and even bridges. Then he had me look at a railroad schedule, and compare planed to actual times.

Water tanks were constructed for the steam engines about every ten to twenty miles. These tanks were normally made of wood and held together with rows of long iron bars that wrapped all the way around the tank. Iron bar rows were close together near the bottom of the tanks, then farther apart near the top. They all seemed to leak a little, but this loss of water was small. Each water stop had a name. I chuckled at the names given these stops. Some were sure to become towns.

Once when we were traveling west out of Omaha I made a list of the water stops. They were; Valley, Fremont, North Bend, Columbus, Clarksville, Grand Island, Kearney Junction, Elm Creek, Plum Creek, Willow, Brady, Maxwell, North Platte, O'Fallon's, Alkali, Ogallala, Big Spring, Barton, Denver Junction, Chapel, Sidney, Potter, Dix Bushnell, and Pine Bluff. My Father said that some would become important towns or cities. However, then, they were just sites on the wind swept prairie. Once the railroads were stretched across the plains, it was amazing how fast the land became occupied.

Boy, those passenger cars are uncomfortable, especially during long night rides. When the cars were crowded, which was often, the seats were often fully occupied, and some passengers even had to stand. For a young fellow like me, I just stretched out on the floor on a blanket and slept. In the summer, when the windows were open, some of the smoke from the engine always came drifting into the passenger cars. The soot, especially as the engines were switching from wood to coal fuel, seemed to get in your eyes, and even into your skin. One night our train was robbed, or, I should say that an attempt was made.

CHAPTER 3
ATTEMPTED TRAIN ROBBERY

Boom!   A gun went off in our passenger car; the sound reverberated through the passenger car, a woman screamed, then another. Dimly lit, with only two small lamps, one at each end of the car, the passenger coaches did not allow reading or games. From under the seat, and through the legs of the other passengers, I could see a man leaning against the door at the far end of our car. Blood oozed down the front of his shirt every time he took a breath. He coughed once, then, quit breathing.

Crawling to the aisle, looking down toward the door, I could see Tex, with his pistol in his hand, standing over this fellow. He blew the smoke from his pistol's barrel. I heard another gun shoot. This second shot caused Tex to jump to the dying robber, shove him out of the way of the door, and go out on the walkway between the passenger cars.

The train was slowing down, and I heard a third shot. Then silence. I looked around the car at the passengers. Most of the men were looking at the car door that Tex had gone through. A few had stuck their heads and weapons out of windows, and the women, both of them, had squirmed down in their seats, like they were trying to become as small as possible. My Father looked down at me, and said,

"Stay where you are Luke." I did!

It seemed like it was a long time, but it could not have been more than a few minutes, when the Conductor came into our passenger car. He walked directly to the dead man, looked down, then, turning to face the passengers. He said,

"Ladies and gentlemen, we have just experienced an attempted hold-up. None of the passengers have been harmed."

The train began to move faster again, and I looked a question at my Father. Who shook his head no! The conductor then moved to the middle of the car, and said,

"We owe Tex our gratitude for his quick thinking, and shooting. His shot seemed to have rattled the other two robbers, as the shot had obviously come from this passenger car. The other shots you heard, downed another of the outlaws, and one other outlaw was seen racing away from the train on a horse." After a pause he said,

"We will be coming into a station in just a little while."

Pointing to the body, he continued,

"There we will dispose of this outlaw and the other one also. We will probably have to wait for the local lawman, and we will send a telegram to our headquarters. If you would like to get off and stretch, I suspect we will be there for about a half an hour."

My Father asked,

"Can you describe what happed?" The conductor looked around at the passengers, and could see that they all wanted to know. The Conductor, said,

"I do not know all of the details, but if you want I will tell you what I think happened." Everyone nodded assent.

"There were probably three outlaws, and possibly a forth that held their horses. They must have jumped on the train back a ways when we were slow coming up the grade. One came into this car, a second went into the other passenger car, and a third outlaw, began banging on the Express car, trying to get the agent to let him in."

Turning to Tex, he said,

"Tell us what happened here." Tex said,

"This here fellow," waving toward to the body that now had been covered with a blanket, "Came through the door, with his pistol in his hand. As he was taking a look around, I drew and fired, and he slid down the door."

The Conductor smiled, and continued,

"A second outlaw, in the other passenger car, had the passenger's with their hands held high. He jumped when he heard Tex's shot. Shortly thereafter, he backed to the connecting car door, probably to see what had happened to his fellow outlaws. Another cowboy in that car drew and shot that outlaw as he turned to exit the car door. The third outlaw must have leaped off the train just as it slowed. A possible fourth, outlaw, or horse-holder brought him a horse and they raced way into the night. Mind you, that is the way I think it happened, but at the next station, I will be speaking to each passenger about the attempted robbery."

Everyone began to talk, telling each other what they had seen. My Father indicated that I should, get-up off the floor and sit next to him. Father asked if I had any questions. I nodded yes, and asked,

"How did that cowboy, uh Tex, know it was an outlaw when he came through the door?"

He replied,

"Luke, in this part of the west, one does not enter a room, pointing with a pistol in his hand, unless he is up to no good."

About noon the next day, we arrived in Denver. It was very nice to sleep in a bed again. Denver was a fast growing town; and was often referred to as the

Rocky Mountain High town. Gold and other minerals were mined in several places to the west; and resulted in Denver being their supply point. Father had to see some people about work, so I had the run of the hotel. The hotel was not as plush as the one where we had stayed in St. Louis, but it beat sleeping on the floor of a railroad car. I went to the restaurant, and had a great breakfast; they even had a special treat, fresh eggs!

One can get a good feel for the local situation of a town by just sitting on a hotel porch and watching the traffic. I took a straight-backed chair and watched the parade of wagons, buggies, people on horseback and the fast striding individuals in a hurry to some place. I was startled when someone addressed me by name. Looking up, into set of very clear blue eyes of a man, I noted that he was wearing a badge on his vest.

He asked,

"Are you Luke?" I said

"Yes Sir."

"You were on the train last night when the robbery attempt was made?"

"Yes Sir"

"This is what I have been told." and he recounted the event almost exactly as the Conductor had related it.

Then he asked,

"Can you add anything else to the story?"

I sat there for a minute, then, said,

"I was asleep on the floor when Tex fired his pistol, killing that outlaw. So I did not see very much, as I had to look through several pairs of legs."

The lawman smiled, but said nothing. I continued,

"I was wondering how the outlaws got on the train, all at the same time, and why the train kept going, even after the first shot was fired? But, then slowed down, right where the fellow was holding the getaway horses?"

The lawman looked at me for some time, then took a chair next to mine, and said,

"Luke, those are d- - - good questions. Questions that makes one wonder!"

As we sat there, my Father came walking up, and having already met the lawman, he took a seat. The lawman, then turned to Father and said,

"Bill, I have just been talking to Luke about the train robbery attempt, and he has asked a very interesting question."

Then he retold what I had told the Marshall. Father, looked at me, smiled, and said,

"I have been trying to teach Luke to be observing. To look and see and remember." Smiling, he said, "It must be working."

The lawman smiled, stood, and said,

"Well, Luke has given me something to look into." Then he walked off down the street. My Father looked at me and asked,

"Do you know who that was?" I shook my head no. He said,

"That is US Marshal David Cook. You need to remember his name, because he will be an important man in the future of law in this area. Already he is forming a Rocky Mountain Detective Association." After that had sunk into my brain, Father said,

"Tomorrow we will be going south on the Denver & Rio Grande line to Littleton, Colorado, not far south of here."

CHAPTER 4
NABBING AN OUTLAW

Father and I sat on the hotel porch watching the Denver traffic for about an hour, then Father pulled out his watch, looked at it and said,

"Luke, I have an appointment in a few minutes. I do not think it will take long, but stay around the hotel."

I nodded, and soon noticed a fellow on horseback, all bent over like he was hurting bad, riding a worn-out horse. I thought, 'That horse will be glad to see the livery'. He wove through the traffic, and to my surprise, rode right-by the livery. I stood up, and out of curiosity, I watched him turn in at a dry-goods store. He practically fell of his horse. He paused and stood almost leaning against his horse then, with difficulty, started to climb the stairs to the second floor.

Now my curiosity was really triggered. So, I walked down the street to see just where he was going. When I got abreast of the dry-goods store, I saw a sign that said, "Doctor up Stairs."

As I walked back to the hotel porch, I wondered about why that fellow was seeing the doctor. I turned around and walked back to the fellow's horse. That horse was exhausted; head drooping, gasping for breath and oblivious to everything around him. As I approached that horse, I could see blood on its' saddle.

Well, I said to my self, he must be hurt, and strolled back to the Hotel porch. Oh yes, I did take a winding course back through the traffic. You, see, there were a couple of nice looking girls, looking at me out of the back of a wagon. I simply had to keep pace with them. When it passed the hotel, I climbed the porch steps, and resumed my seat in that straight-backed chair.

I suppose I was napping, because I did not see Marshall Cook come upon the porch. He nudged me, and I almost fell out of my chair. He laughed, then I laughed, and he sat down. After a short pause he asked,

"Luke, I don't suppose you have seen that third outlaw riding by?"

That remark struck a cord and I said,

"Maybe!"

The marshal looked at me smiling, then, he asked,

"Are you serious?"

I told him about me seeing the fellow who rode by a while ago, and what I had seen. The Marshall asked,

"I suppose that fellow is still in the Doctor's office?"

"I can still see his horse standing in front of the Doctor's office."

"Do you know where my office is?

No!

He told me where it was and asked me to go there quickly, and to send his' Deputy to the Doctor's office.

I took off at a run. Unnoticed by the many people on the move along the main street, breathlessly, I barged into the Marshall's office, but no one was there. I turned around, went back outside, and stood looking up and down the street for the Deputy.

Someone asked,

"Are you looking for the law?"

I gasped a short,

"Yes sir!" He smiled and said,

"I just saw him in the bank."

The bank was just across the street and up a few doors, so I took off again. He was just coming out of the bank, when, I, gasping for breath, told him that the Marshall, wanted him urgently at the Doctor's office. He looked at me a moment, like, maybe he thought this may be some sort of a joke. However, he could see that I was serious, and taking large strides headed across the street.

I was standing there gasping for breath when a fellow in a fancy suit, blocked my line of sight to the Doctor's office. I moved to get my line of sight back, when he too moved in front of me. I had to look at him.

He said,

"Young man, what is going on?" Taking a big breath, I said,

"Police business." Then I began my stroll back to the Hotel, glancing at the Doctor's office every few seconds. I saw the Deputy climb the stairs, draw his revolver, and enter the Doctor's office.

Waiting for I do not know what (a blasting revolver, a cry of help or braking glass, or something), but nothing happened. Nevertheless, my imagination was running a bit wild, as I pictured a serious operation in progress, or something like it. When I got to a position where my next step would cause me to loose sight of the door to the Doctor's office, I stalled for a few minutes.

Finally, I continued on to the Hotel and resumed my seat. It must have been an hour later, I saw the Deputy appear at that fellow's horse, and lead it to the livery. In about ten minutes the Deputy, reappeared and went back to the Doctor's office.

Now my imagination was really running wild. I had thoughts of the outlaw (I assumed that he was one of the train robbers) as holding the Marshall at gunpoint, and had forced the Deputy to take his horse to the livery.

However, that did not make sense, so I thought, "The doctor is performing an operation to extract a bullet from the outlaw, saving his' life so he can be hung."

That too did not have a ring of truth to it. 'I then supposed that he had been hurt in an accident, had ridden miles to see the doctor, and the Marshall was assisting the Doctor in treating that fellow.'

I decided that that last vision was the most likely scenario. It was getting on to lunchtime so I went in to the restaurant and ordered a sandwich and glass of milk. While eating, I noticed a Drummer, at another table, displaying some new Colt pistols to a fellow. I listened to the sales message the Drummer had memorized, and walked over to look at the new pistols. The Drummer had a wide selection of revolvers, and just laying those out on a table caused a small crowd to gather.

The Drummer became a bit agitated when he noticed that I was standing there. I think he was feeling guilty about having mouthed such a big sales pitch. So, I went back outside to my chair on the porch. I fanaticized my self with two of those fancy colts in two holsters, fitted around my waist for a cross draw, a - - , but Marshall Cook sat down next to me in a chair.

Darn! He interrupted my vision of me as a gunfighter. Oh! Well! The Marshall asked,

"Have you caught any more outlaws this morning?" I blushed, and shook my head no.

He said,

"Well you are wrong Luke." I looked at him. He was smiling. I did not know what to say so I just looked at him, and waited.

The Marshall was looking down the street, and I followed his gaze. He was watching Father come up the street to the hotel. He too, came upon the porch, and took a chair.

Then the Marshall said to Father,

"Your son has been catching outlaws this morning." I, and Father, looked questioningly at Marshall Cook.

"Luke, here, noticed a fellow, who appeared to be injured, ride by on his way to the Doctor's office. Just to follow-up, I had Luke fetch my Deputy. We went to the Doctor's office and found there, the third outlaw. The one that was wounded in the recent attempted train robbery."

"He had a pretty bad wound in his left shoulder, and the Doctor enlisted my Deputy and me, to assist in an operation to extract the bullet in his shoulder. The bullet had broken one of the major arteries near the outlaw's heart. Well to make a long story short he died, but before he died, he confessed to the train robbery attempt."

"That takes care of the outlaws, now we need to enlist Detective Luke's services in locating and nabbing the horse holder for the robbery."

He began to laugh, and Father and I joined in the Hee Haws.

Then he said,

"Oh yes, I suspect there will be a reward for at least one of the outlaws, so Luke will have to split the reward with that cowboy named Tex, if we can locate him?"

I think passers-by must have thought we were a bit loony, sitting there on the Hotel front porch laughing our heads off.

CHAPTER 5
GOING TO KANSAS CITY

It was only a bit over ten miles to Littleton, but the engine on our train chugged along, at only about ten to fifteen miles per hour, stopping several times to pick-up and drop-off passengers and freight; it took almost two hours for the trip. Even so, that is much shorter than an all day trip in a wagon.

On the way, Father seemed unusually talkative, and evidently, while we were in Denver had been in a discussion on Buffaloes. It seems that recent federal estimates were that hunters were killing Buffaloes at a rate of about three million each year, and many people were trying to get the government to stop this slaughter before the Buffalo were exterminated.

Father said that the Congress had sent a law to the President that would protect the Buffalo herd. However, President Grant had vetoed the law. Now, wagers were being made on when the last Buffalo would be killed. I could tell that my Father was somewhat upset, but was at a loss as to what could be done. He reckoned that, someday people would look back and recognize the tragedy that was currently unfolding.

I had some difficulty understanding how "All" of the Buffalos could possibly be killed." Many times when riding the rails, the train had to stop so that a literal sea of Buffalo could cross the tracks. The problem with Buffalo herds is they tend to either slow walk when traveling, or stampede. Stampedes are bad, because they run over and through anything in their way; even trains had been damaged by stampeding buffalos.

My Father then turned the conversation to our trip to Littleton, and the large flour mill we would see there. It was named the 'Rough and Ready Flourmill', which had a capacity to grind wheat to flour at a great rate. Owners of the mill were contemplating the possibility of shipping their flour to the eastern states.

A center-vent turbine water wheel provided the mill's power, which generated 32 horsepower for grinding wheat. Although, in January, a few months ago, the mill had burnt down, now it had been rebuilt. It was a very large building, being some 45x64 feet and five stories high. Called 'Little, Lilley & Company', they had received several orders for large quantities of their flour.

To support this order, knocked-downed barrels were being shipped from Kansas City, to fulfill a large flour order for Boston. A full 20,000 bushels of wheat was on hand with another 40,000 bushels available locally. My Father was coordinating this enterprise for the several railroads involved.

It was while we were in Littleton that I discovered we would also be going next to Boston. I was excited and at the same time defensive about going back east. Yes, I would like to see the sights, but the days and days of riding the rails, I dreaded.

On our trip east, Father called my attention to a news article about a fellow named Joseph Glidden. It said that he had received a patent for a barbed wire that was inexpensive, durable, and effective in the fencing of cattle. My Father asked,

"Luke, what will this invention do to ranching?"

I replied,

"The first thing it will do is change the cowboys' life." He nodded his head, and said,

"Yes, if it works it will certainly change their lives. And if it does as well as this article indicates, it could spell the demise of them all." I did not like that kind of talk. I felt that we needed cowboys just as we needed Buffaloes.

We spent a few days in Kansas City and visited the very large stockyards. It was amazing to see the thousands of cattle processed through Kansas City. One day, Father took me to a slaughterhouse. It was terrible! The smell, I do not think I will ever forget. Afterwards, he said,

"Perhaps you were a bit young to see that, but it is part of one of the largest industries in the US, and you need to know what it is all about."

It was my first time to see the new tall buildings, some as tall as seven stories. One night, my Father took me to a real opera house that had stage shows. I had attended some local melodramas, but this was a real professional production.

I was amazed at the jugglers, sword shallower, knife throwers and trained animals. I wondered how they taught those animals to do such tricks. A later act was some large lady, with a matching voice, who sang in a foreign language. That was not good! I preferred the Boo! Hiss shows, where you did not have to interpret what was going on. Nevertheless, it was fine entertainment, and night to remember.

Chapter 6
A Pullman Car

From Kansas City to St. Louis, we rode in a new Pullman Car. It was plush, with a toilet and most everything else. There was even dining facilities, where you could sit down, order, and eat a meal. In addition, at night they had pull-down bunks for sleeping. Amazing!

Railroaders were also talking about another Pullman Concept called the Emigration Car. Built in California, it was constructed so that back-to-back seating converted to two upper and two lower berths each 2ft. 8in wide and 5ft 9in long. These berths were just the basics of a bed, but surely better than sitting up all night.

There were few children traveling east on these trains, but those to whom I had a chance to talk to, thought that I was extremely lucky to have traveled the west. They said,

"West," like, it was heaven. When I told of the train robbery, they would not believe it. One mother sought out my Father, and affronted him for letting his son tell such wild tales. When Father affirmed the story, that mother said,

"Humpf", and stalked off.

I did make one good friend, his name was Moses, and he was what they called a "Porter." He was quiet, unassuming, and seemed to enjoy my company. When I told him about the train robbery, he said,

"We dasen't hav sech here in th east." I found out later that he had been a bronco buster (The fellow that breaks wild horses for riding). When I pressed him to tell me about busting broncos, he smiled and leaned back.

He began, "Onct, I wes woking a train out a Wyomin, when a coupl a cattlemen gets into a discus about wild hoses. One declared that there wus nar a hoss' that coldn't be rid. Tuther feller declared that evry hoss cold be rid. Purty soon, they wus a betten on this, and one said that he has a hoss that no one could rid. Tuther feler says, "Bet ya hunnerd smakers, I knows som'n who kan.""

"Weel, they stopps th train, and I rids that bronc, till he jest stands thr a gaspin for air.'

'Thhe feller who wins, slipps me five o'them five dollar gold coins. Best money I'v evr made ah ridin."

We left St. Louis and crossed the Mississippi River just as the sun was coming up. Man! That is one wide river. It made me feel a bit woozy on that long, high bridge. From then on, the countryside got crowded. You just could not see a bit of open space. It seemed there was a farmhouse and barn on every section of land, some time more than one.

Once, as I was nosing around, I looked down to see that two fellows were handcuffed together. I stopped and looked for a few seconds, but felt embarrassed, and rushed back to our seats and told Father what I had seen. He said,

"Yes, I have seen that before. I assume that it is a US Marshall transporting a criminal to someplace." I must have asked several more questions when he said,

"Luke, just go ask them, be polite, and explain what you want to know. If they will not or can not tell you, they will tell you so."

It took me a while to get up the courage, but I did go back there, and asked about the handcuffs. One of them was a Deputy US Marshall, and he was transporting a prisoner. The prisoner, arrested in a different state than the one where he committed a crime, was being returned for trial.

I asked,

"What would you do if your prisoner tried to escape?" He looked at his prisoner, then at me, grinned, and said,

"I would shoot him." That ended my questions.

The next day a section of track was being repaired from some sort of accident. Our train had to stop, and passengers were allowed out to stretch. I was looking at the engine, big machinery like that seemed to grab my attention. Then I heard a shot.

Looking toward the rear of the train, everyone else was craning to look also. I gulped, when I saw that US Marshall, come walking up to the Conductor taking a handcuff off his left wrist. I think I knew what had happened. As I suspected, the criminal had used the stopping of the train to attempt an escape from the Deputy Marshall. How he got out of the handcuffs puzzled me a bit, so I searched for the Marshall to ask.

He said,

"The criminal asked to be released to relieve himself, so I unlocked his hand cuff. Then, he took off running. I yelled for him to stop. He didn't. So I stopped him."

That is all he would say, I wanted to know more, but the train whistle was blasting away. "All-A-Board," Yelled the Conductor, and then, the train jerked, and, began to move along. I had to jump to grab a handle to swing myself up onto the steps. I sat catching my breath and told Father about the US Marshal's prisoner. Father changed the subject and asked,

"Have you noticed that the clothes people wear going east are different than those going west. I looked around, but shook my head no. Father said,

"Most folks are sensitive about fitting into society, and want not to be looked down on. However, men from the west care little about their clothes, like that fellow two seats in front of us."

I got up walked the length of the car and returned. Having it called to my attention, I noticed that a passenger from the west, often sat by himself. I mentioned that to Father, who smiled and said,

"I believe the westerner wears a different type of perfume." Then we both chuckled.

Chapter 7
Lost

Several times, we had to change trains, some because it was the end of that particular railroad's tracks, and some because the train did not go toward our destination. Most railroad Depots were very large and crowded; I had to stay very close to my Father. Then it happened!

Whether it was a change in tracks for our train, or if I just misunderstood, I will never know. Father and I had made a pact, that if while traveling we were ever separated; we were to go to the dining or club car and wait.

There I sat in the dining car, waiting patiently for my Father to arrive. Often, I had to wait more than an hour for him to arrange for our baggage and sleeping bunks.

After almost an hour, they had a clock in the dining car; a waiter came to me and asked if I was going to order lunch. I said,

"I am waiting for my Father."

He nodded and went away. I had the eeriest feeling. Looking around the dining car, I did not see even one person that I recognized. This was unusual, because there were other people going to Boston that I had previously seen.

About the time I was ready to find the Conductor, the waiter returned, and asked if he could be of assistance. I explained about our pact to meet in the dining car if we became separated, but I had not seen any of the other people going to Boston. He, got a startled look on his face and said,

"This train does not go to Boston!"

I said,

"I think that I had better go talk to the Conductor."

The waiter said,

"Let me see if I can locate him?"

For what seemed like a long time, I sat there in a sort of a stupor, not knowing what to do. I suppose that I looked like I was going to break out bawling. An older lady came to the table and sat down. She was accompanied by the waiter, and he introduced her as Mrs. Scott, a widow."

Before she could ask a question, I blurted out my problem, my Father, my baggage and how I felt marooned. By the time I had ran through my miseries, the Conductor arrived. He was a bit stuffy, and right away, hinted that I might be a stowaway, just looking for a free ride. That did it; I flat out began to bawl.

Right in the middle of this, the Conductor stood and called out,

"Next stop St. Louis, in about one hour." Immediately I began to bawl again, sobbing, I said,

"We were in St. Louis yesterday!"

After I calmed down some, the Conductor took my name and my Father's name, and said he would send a wire at the next stop, and see if my Father could be located. Mrs. Scott offered to buy me a sandwich and glass of milk. I accepted, as I was famished.

Just as I was downing the last of a very good sandwich, the Conductor returned, and asked,

"Could you spell your last name? I said, "MARKANIS."

"And your Father's first name?"

"Bill. Uhh William."

He turned to leave when Mrs. Scott, asked,

"Do you suppose he is the Bill Markanis who works for several railroads?"

The Conductor said,

"I was wondering about that my self, and it is the reason I came back to make sure that I had the name right."

With some food in my stomach, and the shock wearing down, I leaned my head on the table and went to sleep.

When I awoke the train was slowing down for a water stop, and looking out the window in the dark, I saw the Conductor hand a piece of paper to the station telegrapher. In just a few minutes, the train whistle blew, and we were on our way again.

Mrs. Scott asked if I would like to come to her seat and keep her company until we arrived in St. Louis. It seemed the thing to do, so I nodded; still afraid that I might start bawling again if I talked. I sat, leaned, squirmed, and finally passed out, awaking only when we were coming into the station at St. Louis.

The Conductor came by and said to Mrs. Scott,

"I hesitate to ask, but could you accompany Luke for a few minutes, while I clear the train and check to see if there is a reply to the telegram I sent?"

I felt like a fool, a very lonesome fool. She agreed, and I assisted her in carrying some of her carry-on bags off the train. As we entered the terminal building, standing there was a fellow in a very neat uniform.

He was more than a little shocked, but Mrs. Scott said,

"Jenkins, we will need a place in the lounge for a few minutes." It obviously took some seconds for Jenkins to digest what Mrs. Scott had said, and accept the presence of a young lad in tow, one he had never seen before, then he replied,

"Yes Ma'am."

Turning to a fellow with a red cap, he signaled for him to stay with the bags, and he took Mrs. Scotts' arm, and led us to a very nice VIP Lounge; that is what the sign on the door glass said. I followed along with my small bag.

Wow! That lounge was something else! Carpets that felt like they were coming up over the ankles, a chandelier large enough to bless a ball room, deep, deep cushioned chairs and tables with snacks and reading materials, and a pretty young lady in what I later discovered was a waitresses dress. It was a bit like I had pictured heaven.

I looked at Mrs. Scott then at Jenkins. She was being seated, and he was standing about two paces to her left, and pretty much stiff as a board. Mrs. Scott smiled and said,

"Luke this is my chauffer, Jenkins."

Then turning to Jenkins, she said,

"Jenkins, perhaps you should see to the carriage, we may be here for a short while."

With a sharp little bow, he turned and marched out the door. I have to admit, I had never seen the like. I do remember that a schoolteacher once described such, but I thought that such goings on were only with European Royalty. Mrs. Scott turned to me and asked,

"Luke, would you tell me about your mother?"

Dang, I wish she had not asked that. My tear ducts rapidly filled and threatened to overflow. Somehow, I kept them in check and gave her some of my sweetest memories. Once I got going, I ripped right along, losing track of time. I did note later that Jenkins returned, and resumed his position.

I came back to the present, when the door to the lounge opened and the Conductor came in. You could see that he felt a bit out of place in the VIP lounge, but he walked right up to Mrs. Scott and said,

"We have heard from Mr. Markanis, he has gotten off the train in Philadelphia and will wait there for Luke. I have checked the schedules, and the next direct train will depart at 10:00 am tomorrow morning."

She sat there a minute, taking that all in, then the Conductor, continued,

"If you like, I can see to Luke for tonight, and get him on the correct train tomorrow."

CHAPTER 8

SLEEPING IN A MANSION

Mrs. Scott cleared her throat and said,

"That is very nice of you, but I believe I will see to Luke tonight, and Jenkins and I, will see that he is on the train tomorrow."

The Conductor, said,

"Yes Ma'am. I have arranged for tickets and a voucher. They will be ready by 9:00 am tomorrow morning at the ticket counter."

I do not know why I looked at Jenkins, but I did, and he winked – staying stiff as a board.

Coming out of the terminal there stood the red-capped fellow. Mrs. Scott placed a coin in his hand, and Jenkins gave her a hand up into the carriage. I followed. Jenkins got up on the drivers seat, and a matched pair of white horses trotted off. We were not very far from the terminal; when we turned in to a vine covered archway. Going up a slow rising, curving bricked drive; we approached the front of this very fancy hotel.

As soon as the carriage stopped, another person, in a sort of uniform, helped Mrs. Scott out of the carriage, and he even took my hand as I got down.

Large double doors opened to a hallway, where stood a lady in a uniform. I, of course, was mesmerized, with eyes as big as saucers, trying to take it all in. Mrs. Scott turned to the other servant and said,

"William, will you see that Luke is made comfortable in the blue room."

It was then that I realized this was her home!

William took my small bag and led me up a long curving staircase. I noted that the banister was made just right for a boy to slide down. The blue room was aptly named. The walls were covered in blue velvet looking fabric, and the room was the size of a house. Mirrors on the wall and a very large bed dominated the room.

William, waving his arm at a door said,

"The facilities are here." This, I had never seen before. A toilet one could eat off the floor and not have to worry about catching something. Next, William, went to a very large bed, turned down the covers, and fluffed the pillow. Then turning to me, he asked,

"Will there be anything else?"

I shook my head no, and he went out the door, and shut it with a 'Click.'

That sound was ominous, so I went and opened the door, just to make sure that I had not been locked-in. It was such a grand room, that I did not think I would be able to sleep. That was the last I remembered.

I awoke with a start – looking up at a thing-a-ma-gig that covered the bed like a tent with no sides. Then it started to come back to me. Mrs. Scott, Jenkins, William and the grand house/mansion where I had slept. The clock beside the bed said that it was after 6 am, time to get up.

I almost didn't use the toilet, afraid that I would somehow get it dirty. I did wash the sleep out of my eyes, straightened my clothes, and toured the room. I did not touch a thing; it all looked so expensive. Cautiously I opened the door to exit the blue room. I heard nothing and saw no one. Looking around, I decided that the kitchen would be down stairs. Yes! Then, I slid down the banister. Whee! That was great. I thought about going back up and sliding down again, but decided that I had probably already violated some house rule.

In the entryway, I could hear some activity down a hall that went away from the front door. Easing along, gazing at large paintings, of old, probably dead people, I approached a door without a doorknob. Pushing on the door, it easily swung open, revealing a gleaming white kitchen.

Two ladies were busy doing something. I just stood there watching for a few minutes, before they noticed me. Then they stopped what they were doing, and just starred at me. I was about to bolt back to the bedroom, when the older lady asked. "Are you Luke?"

I nodded.

"Are you hungry?

I nodded.

The two ladies looked at each other; one shrugged her shoulders, then, said,

"Why don't you come and sit at this table, and we will prepare you some breakfast?"

There was a small gleaming white table in one corner of the kitchen; I went to it and sat down. One of the ladies opened a large door, took out a bottle of milk, and filled a glass, then brought it to the table. I said,

"Thank you."

They both looked at each other, and smiled. Soon the aroma of bacon and eggs began to make my taste buds squirt. I had finished about half of the glass of milk, when William came into the kitchen. He seemed startled, but the ladies just looked at him and smiled.

I said,

"Mr. William, won't you join me for breakfast? Such emotions I have never seen passed through his face. He just stood there. Then with a smile and a shrug of his shoulders, he came and sat down. The two ladies giggled.

A heaping serving of bacon, eggs, and bread were brought to the table on a large plate. Boy, it looked good. I sat waiting for a plate for William, when the older lady brought another heaping plate of food to William. I had just stuck my fork into those eggs, when everything, and everyone froze, and it became silent. I looked up to see Mrs. Scott standing at the swinging door, looking at all of us.

She only paused for a moment, then, asked,

"Luke, may I join you and William for breakfast?"

I stood, as William also did, and said,

"Yes Ma'am."

The kitchen ladies giggled again. After Mrs. Scott and William had sat down, she waved for us to continue with breakfast. The ladies must have known what she ate for breakfast, because they did not ask what she wanted. Then she looked at me and asked,

"Did you try sliding down the banister?"

It got quiet. I said,

"Yes Ma'am." She laughed, and the ladies' giggled, and even William smiled. That broke the ice, and while William and I ate our breakfast, she said,

"Luke I have laid out some clothes on your bed, they are some that belonged to my son, who is now a grown man. Since you will be on the train for the next few days, perhaps you would like to take a bath before we go to the station."

I nodded. I could not tell if that was a question, suggestion, or a directive, but I would not have disappointed her for anything. As soon as I had eaten my fill, I excused myself, saying

"I will go bathe now." and departed.

It was an enormous tub, plenty of hot water and some very nice scented soap. I washed all over, even my ears, dried off, and donned the clothes lying on the bed. They fit good, and were of great quality. I began to worry how I was going to pay for this hospitality.

Chapter 9
Going East Again

I went to the kitchen to thank the ladies for the fine breakfast. They giggled some more. I shook Williams hand as we were about to get into the carriage. Jenkins winked at me, while he helped Mrs. Scott in to the carriage.

We were at the station in plenty of time. At the Depot, Jenkins went to the Ticket Window and retrieved the tickets and voucher. Mrs. Scott explained that I could use the voucher in the dining car and for any thing else that I needed on the train. Then she said,

"Your train goes straight through to Philadelphia. They may change engines or such, but you just need to stay on the train. Jenkins and I will go on the train with you to assure that you have an assigned sleeper on the Pullman."

"Do you have any questions?" I thought, and asked,

"How does the voucher work?" She smiled and said,

"You use it like money. Instead of giving money for purchases, you give them the voucher number." Then she showed me the number of my voucher.

I could tell that it was about time to board the train so I blurted out,

"Mrs. Scott you have a grand house, and I want to thank you for your hospitality. And, I want you to know that I slid down the banister again before we left."

That was the only time I saw her laugh. Then with a misty eye she said,

"It has been a long time since we have had a child in our home. You have blessed us far more than you know. Luke, I want you to know, that if you are ever in St Louis, you will always be welcome in my home." Woops, my tear ducts were starting to leak; I threw my arms around her and gave her a big hug.

I had boarded so many trains, that one more was lost to my mind. I do remember shaking William's hand. He put his hand on my shoulder and said,

"Luke, you have benefited us more than you will ever know."

Then I was alone again; alone but with a number of other people all around. With those new, fancy clothes, I felt like everyone was looking at me. It may have been the other way around. When the conductor came by, he called me by name, which caused several passengers to stare at me. I asked for a railroad schedule.

I was sitting in a seat by my self, when a person about my age came down the aisle, and stopped. I looked up. He looked at me for a few moments, and asked,

"Do you want to play some checkers?"

I could not think of any reason not to, and said, Ok."

"I will go and get them." He turned and went back the way he had come. When he came back, his mother was with him. She eyed me for a moment, and asked,

"Are you traveling alone?" I nodded yes.

Then she asked, "Where are you going?"

I told her, and I could see that she was about to veto our checkers game, so I blurted out,

"My Father and I became separated. I am to meet him in Philadelphia." She looked at her son, and nodded approval.

We borrowed a small valise from a fellow traveler, set up the board, and began playing. I looked up when the Conductor came by with a woman, and saw that his' mother was checking on me. I suppose all was well, because she sat back down.

This fellow was a pushover. I won several games then I let him win one. We got bored at checkers and I asked him where he was from. He was well spoken, said that his name was Thomas, that he lived in St, Louis, and he and his mother were going to Chicago to visit his grandparents. Then he began to tell me of how great it was to be living in St. Louis, right on the western frontier.

He then asked if I had ever shot a gun. I nodded yes. Then he went into a long drawn-out story about hunting Geese along the Mississippi River. They had a retrieving dog, and he raved about how it would jump into the water and bring back the dead Geese.

This I was interested in, because several times I had watched great flocks of Geese flying over the wheat fields of Kansas. I had suggested to my Father that we hunt the Geese, but he just said,

"Someday!"

I asked about training a dog to be a retriever. Evidently, he knew little of this, because he had not been involved in training their dog. When I asked what type of guns he had shot, it seemed to be limited to shotguns. Time flew by as we discussed several other topics, when his mother stood in the aisle by our seat.

She said,

"Thomas, it is time to have lunch." He looked at me, I looked at his mother, she, was rather pretty. Then she asked,

"Luke, isn't it? Why don't you join us in the dining car?"

I nodded, and got up and followed them through the next car, and into the dining car. It was crowded, and we had to wait a few minutes to be seated. At a table for four, the three of us sat down, and the waiter reminded us that another single passenger might join us.

I ordered a sandwich, and began to look around, wondering if I would see someone, I knew. Before our meals were served, a rather large fellow was seated at our table; he said that his name was Henry Long. I looked at him because I thought I had heard that name before. However, where, escaped me.

As lunch was finished, the waiters were trying to get diners to leave as soon as they had eaten, but Henry said, "When I finish my coffee."

Then, Thomas' mother also ordered coffee. Meanwhile I dug out my voucher to pay for my lunch. Henry laughed, and produced a voucher. Looking at my voucher, he asked,

"Is Bill Markanis your Father?"

I was startled! I said,

"Yes."

Henry then said,

"He is a good friend of mine." I blushed!. Then he said,

"You know, your Father is one of the best railroad engineers I have ever known." I then explained how we had become separated, and where we were to get together again.

Then it happened. KerasssshH! The wheels of the dining car screeched and ground into gravel, the car jolted and bucked a couple of times, rotated to a direction about 40^0 to the tracks, then, leaned way over on its' side to the right. The side we were seated on.

Chapter 10
Getting Out

It was a mad house. Screaming, crying, cursing filled the dining car, along with hot coffee, and foods of all kinds. I was thrown-up against a window on the down side, and was being held there by some enormous weight. Breathing was difficult, and everyone was coughing and talking or yelling.

I could hardly move, but by turning my head just a little I could see that it was Henry who was on top of me. He too was looking around. Seeing me, he said,

"Luke can you move away from the window, I need to get it open so we can get out."

I said,

"If you can just get off of me a little."

Some kid was bawling in between screams, and yelling for his mother over and over.

Henry grunted, I felt the weight lift off me, and I quickly moved so he could reach the window. With a loud grunt followed by a screech, the window slid open. Then Henry said,

"Luke, drop to the ground, then take the passengers as I hand them out the window."

Hanging on the window frame by my fingers, I could almost reach the ground. Dropping, I discovered that I was standing in the ditch that ran alongside of the railroad tracks. I looked up, and already Henry was handing down a child. It was Thomas, and he was bleeding from a cut over an eye, crying and yelling "Mother, Mother!"

I got him on the ground, and slapped his face. He looked at me, and I pointed to get down the ditch and away from the train. He said, "Mother"

I said,

"Get going, unless you want to die." That got his attention, and he duck-walked along the ditch.

Turning back, Henry was holding a woman by her armpits. I wrapped my arms around her and let her down to the ground. After she pulled her dress down, I pointed her down the ditch. She went stooped over for a few yards, then, assumed the duck-walk position, and I turned back for the next passenger.

It seemed like it took an hour to get every one out of that car. Finally, Henry leaned down and said,

"Get them away from the car, there may be a fire."

That made sense. So I too duck-walked out from under the dining car, to a group of some twenty or more people just standing around, like they thought that by some miracle the rail car would be righted.. They were all talking, so I yelled,

"Get away from the train, there was a cooking fire, and it may spread." I pointed to a fence that ran along the tracks and said,

"Get out to the fence and wait there. There is nothing you can do here but get in the way."

One man, one of the passengers, understood the danger, and began to herd the passengers toward the fence.

I turned back, and duck walked back down the ditch to the train.

Henry looked down at me and said,

"Luke, I have a couple of passengers with broken bones up here. I have explained the situation to them, and they have opted to get out of the train. One has a broken leg, and we will get her out last."

I nodded.

The next passenger was a young girl or woman, and Henry was letting her down, holding on to her chest below the armpits. I grabbed her around the waist, and eased her to the ground. Although she had tears in her eyes, and was holding her broken arm next to her body, she was helpful. I ask if she could go along the ditch by her self. She nodded yes, and began the trip.

Turning back to Henry, I could not see him or a passenger, then, I heard a yelp. Looking around I could see that the girl had fallen, and with a broken arm could not get up.

As fast as I could, I duck walked down to her, got her up, and had her lean on me, until we were clear of the railroad car. One of the men at the fence came to help her. I told him the next passenger had a broken leg, and he said that he would be back to help.

Back at the Dining Car window, Henry had wrapped a couple of strips of cloth around the lady's legs, to hold them together. As she came through the window I did not know how best grab her.

Henry said,

"Luke, see if you can grasp her just below her bottom."

I could, but she was too heavy for me, but just as I was about to collapse, the fellow from the fence took part of the load, and we got her down so she could put her weight on her good leg. Henry said,

"If you'll, just wait a minute, while I check to make sure we have all the passenger out of the car, I will come down and help you."

It seemed like forever, before Henry's legs came through the window. Dropping down, the two men made a sling of their hands for the lady, and kind of duck -walked out from under the rail car.

Finally, standing up, they carried her toward the fence. Some of the passengers came to help, others just stood, like they were in a trance.

A buckboard was coming along the fence to carry the injured to be cared for, then, we heard a Woosh! Turning, we could see that the dining car had begun to burn intensely.

Henry looked at me, and I at him, and he said,

"Just in time, a few more minutes and this would have been a real disaster."

I nodded, and said,

"Henry, I lost my voucher."

He smiled, and said,

"Me too!"

The remainder of that day was almost like a nightmare. Accusations, counter accusations, yelling, pointing of fingers, crying, and large portions of "Thank the Lord." This was my first experience with newspaper reporters.

They were a bit disgusting, asking leading questions wanting to hear their answers. It made one think that they were going to describe what had happened, their own way, regardless of what the passengers on the train were saying.

CHAPTER 11
HEROES

That night I slept on a small Depot's wooden bench, and slept well, too. The next morning I awoke hungry, and when I went to the Depot restaurant, they fed me breakfast, and never asked for a dime. By mid morning, we could see that a work crew was busy repairing the railroad tracks, and then, Henry reappeared. He told me that he had sent a wire to my Father, giving him a summary of yesterday's events. That somewhat eased my anxiety.

A fellow from a newspaper interviewed Henry and I, and asked numerous questions. He kept asking the names of the passengers we helped get out of the dining car, but we knew very few. Later, we heard that the reporters had interviewed the passengers of the dining car, all of which called us real heroes.

Somehow, Henry had obtained Vouchers for him and me, and had gotten tickets for us to continue on our journey. Henry took it on himself to travel with me to Philadelphia, to talk to my Father. As we boarded a replacement train later that day, I saw Tommy. When he saw me, he just nodded, and sat with his mother. After we were on our way, Henry said,

"Luke, I have been asked by the railroad to check on those two ladies that had broken bones. Want to come with me?" I said,

"Sure."

They were a couple of cars back, so we had a long walk down the aisles. I noticed several people eyeing us as we passed them. The lady with the broken leg had it up on the facing seat. It was all wrapped up, with splints down each side. She was in a little pain, but very kind with her thanks. The lady, with a broken arm, grabbed me with her good arm and began to cry.

I did not know what to do. Finally, she said,

"Luke, when you came under that car to help me get to my feet, I was so thankful. I just knew that that car was going to fall on me. And when it burst into flames, I could just see me burning to death under there."

I suppose my face turned a bright red; at least that is the way it felt. As we returned down the aisle to our car and seats, the people broke into the song, 'For he's a jolly good fellow.' Henry turned and bowed. I blushed some more.

With a couple of days to become acquainted, Henry and I became good friends. He was a bridge specialist, and was on his way to a large steel mill, to obtain materials for replacing several wooden trestle bridges. He talked long about the capacity of steel to take heavy loads. Then he said,

"You know Luke, almost ten years ago your Father recommended that railroads should go to steel bridging, and only now have the railroads acknowledged that need." He had many nice things to say about my Father.

I thought it odd that a friend knew so many things about my Father; often more than I knew. I began to wonder about Fathers adventures when he was away working on railroads. Prodding Henry a little, he began to talk about Father. His tone was one of wonderment, and he stopped often to think and assure that his memory was correct.

He told of Father going into the Dakotas seeking a railroad route. It being Blackfoot Indian Territory, there was real danger. Henry said,

"Your Father told me of how he was always honest when dealing with the Indians. Everyone else, including our own Government, always made promises that they never kept. William, Bill, made it a point always to tell them, as it would really be. In dealing with the Blackfoot Chief's he had told them that eventually, a rail line would be built into their lands."

"The Blackfoot Indians were very angry, because that would violate their existing treaty. But, your Father said,

"I told them that it does not mater what paper or treaty has been signed, I am telling you that eventually a railroad will come through your lands." Many of the Braves wanted to execute your Father, but the old Chief said,

"I think he tell truth. We need someone who will tell us truth; we hear many lies; many lies."

Your Father said that the Chiefs then held a big Council, asked him many questions, which he answered the best that he could. Often he said,

"This is my best guess as to how the White Man will slowly acquire your land, and it will likely end up with you having to reside on only a small reservation."

As you can imagine, the Blackfoot Indians were very upset. Many wanted immediately go to war, but your Father said, I told them that they had no real chance to win. It would just cause the deaths of many members of their tribes.

After a lengthy pause, Henry continued.

"I can not imagine how your Father got out of there alive. It must have been as if he was sticking a sword in their belly, and having to tell them that there is no other option. However, the Blackfoot Indians thought so highly of your Father, that they sent an escort with him as he made a preliminary survey of a rail route." He said,

"You know Luke; I never thought that he would be able to complete that assignment." Pausing, he then said,

"I do not think anyone in the railroad business thought he would ever return with a preliminary survey. And, the railroad track's, are now being constructed practically on top of his' survey."

"Contrary to everyone else's thinking, your Father returned to that Indian Council, and sketched out his best estimated of exactly where the railroad would likely be built. Because it crossed some of their special hunting grounds, the young Braves were very upset. But, your Father said,

"I just told them the truth. The tribal Chiefs were also upset, but they seemed to recognize that your Father was telling them the truth."

"When your Father returned to Kansas City and presented his survey to the big Shots, they just shook their heads in wonder. Yes, Luke, your Father is a wonder. Somehow he can see and feel the way to proceed, and can quickly assimilate new ideas and designs into existing systems."

Well, I had to get Henry to tell me what assimilate means, but it was the correct word, and I now had a new word to use.

After an even longer pause, Henry said,

"You should be proud of your Father. He has caused many new techniques and materials to be used, and to the benefit of all the railroads. I suppose you know that when a really difficult problem springs up, almost all railroad owners mention your Father's name first when discussing someone to resolve the issue."

I sat and thought about my Father. I knew he was special, but I had no idea he was also special to other people. Then, I remembered one who 'knew' my Father was special. It was mother, Jane. I suppose that is why she never complained when Father went off on a job.

She knew that his talents could solve the problem, when others would just get in over their heads.

I turned to Henry, and said,

"I suppose that Father is like a Doctor for the railroads." Henry broke into laughter, and said,

"You are more right than you will ever know."

I sat there thinking about causing Father a large concern, by messing up and getting on the wrong train. I said as much to Henry, who said,

"You are still young Luke; just do not ever make the same mistake again." I nodded. This discussion made me proud of my Father, but knowing he disliked being praised; I decided to keep it to myself.

As we sat there thinking, Henry asked,

"Luke, how many railroaders are in this car?" Looking around I counted the Porter, and the Conductor, then said,

"Two."

Henry smiled and said,

"Actually there are four." This time I stood up and looked all around, sat down, and said,

"There are only two, and named them." Henry asked,

"Tell me what items identify a person as a railroader?"

I was puzzled and said,

"I do not understand." Henry chuckled, and said.

"Look two seats toward the back. See that fellow with the gold watch and chain in his vest?" I nodded.

"What kind of watch is that he is wearing?

"A railroad watch!"

I caught on to Henry's question, stood and took a good look around. I saw no more railroad watches. And said,

"I give up who is the other one?"

"Look at the boots of the ruggedly dressed individuals," he said. Just a quick look around and I discovered a big brawny fellow with some well worn boots." I asked,

"Is that fellow in the third row seat, the one?"

"Yes," he said,

"Now tell me, what is his job on the railroad, and tell me if he is right or left handed?"

After a careful look I said,

"He is a fireman, and he is right handed."

"Very good Luke!" Now explain how you made that determination?"

"His boots are very well worn, but the left one has burn scars on the toe. Only a right handed fireman shoveling a lot of coal would have his left boot right at the boiler hopper."

"Well done. Now I wonder if you can tell me where those two railroaders live."

So, the game went on for several hours. It was a real education; there is so much to notice, however we almost constantly discard it without even thinking. Henry was a good teacher, as well as a friend.

Finally, we arrived in Philadelphia, and as I had hoped, there, on the arrival platform stood my Father with open arms. Boy, it felt good to have his arms around me again. I was tired, literally exhausted from the nearly two days of travel without my Father.

After some backslapping, and thanks, my Father suggested that we go to the depot restaurant, so he could hear of our adventures. Henry laughed at that.

I was pleased that Henry wanted me to help tell the tale. In fact, he went at it such that it seemed like I was doing the telling. After the train wreck tale, my Father asked me to review my introduction to Mrs. Scott. He smiled a lot as I recounted our meeting and described her house and servants. Then he said,

"Mrs. Scott is the widow of one of the biggest railroad owners. Every railroader in the USA admires her. She sent me a wire saying that you were a perfect gentleman. I want you to know that I am proud of you."

"I have read the papers about the train wreck, and Henry has confirmed the fact that you really came through during a crisis. And, you need to know, that you are now known up and down the railroad lines as a true railroader."

I blushed. Then I went to sleep when Henry and my Father began to talk about railroad equipment. Tomorrow, we are to continue on to Boston.

After the events of the past few days, I thought that Boston may be boring, but Father was excited about a new invention he had read about in a Boston newspaper. Henry had departed, to visit a steel mill and we boarded a train for Boston. I suppose Father could see that I was a bit bored, so he asked if I knew any of our Country's history of Boston.

I told him that I knew about the Boston Tea Party. He then began to tell me about Paul Revere and the lights used to alert the Minutemen. He used that event to kindle my interest, then spoke of the Revolutionary fighting, Concord, Valley Forge and some of the battles that General Washington fought.

I was surprised to discover that General Washington had lost almost nine battles, before he won the deciding battle; the battle that gave our Nation its' independence. I asked how he knew about those things. He said that there were books that recounted the essential elements of the Revolutionary Ward, the War of 1812, and soon, books would be printed about the Civil War.

I asked if we could get some of these books, and he said that he would try to find some while we were in Boston. I jumped back to the Boston Tea Party, and asked,

"Just what was that all about?"

For several hours, Father talked about things such as taxes, representation, and import duty. I suppose that the most important thing that I discovered was that I knew very little about our government's history. I also discovered, again, that my Father was much wiser than I ever suspected.

He cautioned me not to belittle men, because you never know whom you are talking to, and this was especially true in the west. I had to think on that, which caused me to remember that large flourmill in Colorado. Someone had to know about turbines, marketing and sales.

Our arrival in Boston was uneventful, except at the train terminal. It was large, busy, and fairly dirty. It seemed like coal dust, and grime followed the railroads wherever they went. The next day I was told to stay in or around the hotel as my Father visited people about shipping flour from the west.

Outside the hotel, the first thing I noticed was the finery of the clothes that the Bostonians wore. Almost every woman wore a large hat; these were large and well decorated hats. I wondered how they could get in and out of carriages with such large headpieces. The streets were very crowded, and streetcars, some pulled by mules but most ran using overhead electric, continually passed the hotel. I wanted to take a ride and tour Boston.

Out front on the sidewalk, there was a big shoeshine stand. I watched young boys, and even men clean mud, and other debris, off shoes, and polish them until they had a bright shine. There were no cowboy boots worn. The hotel lobby was clean and well equipped with large, stuffed chairs. For hours I sat and watched the people come and go.

CHAPTER 12
A BIG DEAL

Often a business meeting would be held right next to me. I noted a fellow taking notes on a pad as he listened to some of these meetings. He did not seem to be part of the meeting; essentially, he was eavesdropping. I watched, but could see no action taken, or acknowledgement given to the fellow. I decided to ask Father about him.

That evening at dinner, I asked for permission to ride the streetcars. Father asked where I wanted to go. I said, where ever it goes, I know they make some type of a circuit, because they come by on a regular basis. He thought a minute, then said,

"I think that will be educational," and approved.

Then, I asked about the fellow I saw taking notes in the lobby. He too was curious, and asked that I point him out the next day.

My streetcar ride was very interesting. It went by the site of the Tea Party, and I almost got off, but remembered that the driver had said that if I got off, he would have to charge me another fare. Boston, like many cities had some very posh homes, and some sections of town where the poor lived.

There were many large factories, large mills and when the workday ended, the streets and streetcars were crowded. I decided that I did not want to live in Boston.

Father came back to the hotel earlier than normal, and asked that I, discreetly, point out the fellow who was taking notes. We both sat in comfortable chairs, and watched his actions for about an hour. Then Father went to the fellow and invited him to dinner that evening, saying,

"I am rather new to Boston, and would like to ask a few questions about doing business here. He accepted Father's offer.

Strangely, I too was to be present. After we were seated in the restaurant, the fellow said that his name was John Weeks.

Then Father attacked, saying

"Mr. Weeks, I know what you are doing, although strictly speaking it is not against the law, I believe your activities would not be looked upon with favor by large companies in Boston."

He just starred at my Father. Mr. Weeks became a bit uncomfortable, wiggled around, and was about ready to respond when my Father continued,

"I have a proposal to make to you. I want a copy of your notes weekly. In turn I will provide you a similar set of notes on the railroads of this country, especially those in the west."

"You may not believe in my capabilities, but to demonstrate I will provide you an example."

"I am here in Boston to finalize a deal for a very large flour milling firm in the west. This is a deal with local Boston distributors, to furnish them with all of the flour they can sell."

Mr. Weeks' jaw dropped open. Then it slammed shut. Then he just sat there for several minutes. Then he wrote an address on a sheet of his notebook, and slid it over to my Father. My Father looked at it, nodded, wrote an address on a piece of paper, and slid it across the table to Mr. Weeks, who read it, and nodded.

Then we ordered dinner, and had some polite conversation for about an hour. Mr. Weeks departed, and we went up to our room.

I was anxious to find out about what had happened. In our room, I asked. My Father said,

"Mr. Weeks, sits in the lobbies of the large Boston hotels, and listens. He reads lips, so he often does not have to get very close. Large corporation leaders, often meet on neutral ground, to discuss potential business deals."

"Mr. Weeks, copies down interesting conversations, then, sells his notes to directors of large banks. Then when companies come to these banks, they already have the inside story on deals that are in the making."

I said,

"So, you will give him advance notice of railroad programs, in exchange for Mr. Weeks' notes. Is that legal and above board?"

"Yes, it is above board because the details of pending deals are not disclosed. Just the facts, that people are talking to each other about a deal. This information could probably be obtained from newspapers, but the fact that key players are personally involved, can make the information valuable."

"For example, today I met with a Mr. Westinghouse, about his invention of air brakes for railroad cars. Anyone with a smattering of sense will quickly recognize the need for such a system. Initially, high-level managers will probably resist this system, because it will require a large outlay of money to retrofit every rail car."

However, you and I know that larger engines and longer trains will soon be moving faster and faster. The only way such trains can be stopped is by having good brakes on each and every rail car."

And, what I have just said is exactly what I will give Mr. Weeks in my notes to him next week."

I nodded.

Then Father said,

"We will start our return west tomorrow. We will be making some stops on our return, and maybe we will visit Mrs. Scott. I need to compose a few telegrams to send out tomorrow morning, so why don't you turn in for the night.

I did.

CHAPTER 13
NEW YORK CITY

When the Conductor called our train, I heard him mention New York City. I asked Father if we were going there. He said,

"New York City has become the center of commerce, not only for our country, but the whole world. I have made some contacts there, and I want to personally meet a few of them, before I do any business there."

Father, always an adventurer, arranged for us to ride on a section of a new subway system. A bit scary, it was called, The Beach Pneumatic Transit, it was only a block long, but it was not too difficult to imagine such tubes running to various stations under the city. We boarded the subway for a ride through a dark tunnel, or tube underneath the city. Even the subway cars were like sections of tubes. I did not appreciate the subways potential, until we came back to street level, and observed the dense vehicle and foot traffic.

On the way from Boston, Father had told me that New York was really several cites in one. In sections of New York, called Burroughs, immigrants from particular countries in Europe tended to live next to each other. Thus, the language differences were minimized for business. With whole sections of the city occupied by immigrants from one country, even the shops and restaurants take on the appearance of their homeland. Special foods and baking techniques are evident, as well as celebrations and dances.

He then told me about the Stock Exchange, where as much as a million dollars is traded each day. I asked if he had stocks, and he said,

"Some! I have often received stocks as payment for my work, and some I have purchased. It is often important to hold stock in companies that you work for, because it indicates that you too believe in that company." He also mentioned Wall Street as the center of stock trading. Some very expensive shops and hotels catered to the very rich, and a street named Broadway that contained a large number of entertainment shows.

All the way to New York, I had asked question after question about how stocks and companies fit together. I probably was a bore, but Father answered every question, however, I did not understand every answer. Although, I did gain an understanding of how a company, although appearing like a person, actually contains many people working toward one goal; profits.

Our hotel was comfortable, not flashy, but nice. The next day I wandered around the lobby, visiting the lobby shops, and peeking in on conventions and watching the people. I do believe that New Yorkers are constantly on the run. I found an abandoned book on sailboats in a chair, and curled up for a reading session.

I do not know how long I had been reading before I detected a fellow standing over me. I looked up. He stared at me. I asked,

"Is this your book?"

That question seemed to confuse him. He asked,

"Are you a guest in this hotel?"

"Yes."

"What is your room number?"

I gave it to him and after a few moments, he strode away. I saw him in the lobby again that afternoon, and asked the desk clerk if he was the police?

The clerk giggled, and said,

"He is the House detective.

I must have looked odd, because he said,

"What?" I asked,

"Do you have so many crimes in the hotel that you need your own detective?" That really broke him up. Then he explained that his real duties were to keep the riff raff away from the hotel.

I went back to my sailboat book. The interesting part of this book was how wind-powered sailboats can operate, even when the wind is blowing right at your front. I wondered if it would work on a train on the plains of Kansas.

That evening Father spoke of some lawyers he had seen that day. He just shook his head when I asked questions. He did mention one fellow, a young lawyer not long out of college, who seemed capable and good to know. I forgot his name, but they had discussed some of the stock he owned. He said that he had discovered that currently they were not worth a lot of money.

During the afternoon, I took a seat on the balcony that over looked the lobby, just to watch the people. As I watched, I saw what I thought was a desk clerk slipping money into his pants pockets. He acted a bit guilty, but I thought, maybe I had just imagined it.

Later I definitely saw him take cash from a customer and put it in his pocket. I wondered if this was a job for the house detective. Then I thought I had better first discuss this with my Father. I decided that I would go to the desk and be sure that I knew the clerk's name. I just asked if there was any mail for our room. There was no mail for us, but I read his' name badge, 'Ronald'.

I got to thinking, wondering how many thieves there were in New York City, and how much they obtained by stealing just a few dollars each, each day. For sure, it would amount to a lot of money.

I began to watch the Bell Hops and other hotel staff, to see if everyone was a thief. I did note that the clerk never pocketed any money when the house detective was anywhere in the lobby. I felt like a detective, watching to catch the guilty.

About four pm, a very fancy dressed young lady came into the lobby, followed by two Bell Hops, carrying piles of luggage. As she approached the desk clerk, I saw the house detective signal the desk clerk with a nod of his head.

Although I did not see anything unusual, there seemed to be an air of tenseness that existed until she went up in the elevator. She went to the top floor. I sat there, looking over the rail, wondering what I had missed, when the same lady came out of the elevator, pitched a room key to the clerk, and went out side.

Again, I felt something was amiss, but could not tell what it was. I saw my Father come in, so I ran down the stairs to meet him. We rode the hydraulic elevator up to our room. The hissing and fluid noises were like a sideshow display. As soon as we were in our room, I was telling Father about seeing the Desk Clerk stealing money. This was a serious matter to my Father, and he asked many questions.

He was thinking about my descriptions, when I told him of the pretty lady arriving and the signal that passed between the detective and the Desk Clerk.

It got quiet as my Father contemplated what course of action, if any we should take. Then he jerked, and said,

"I have almost forgotten, we have been invited to dinner. We are to meet my lawyer at a Chinese Restaurant, just down the street at 8 pm."

I wrinkled my nose, as I thought about Chinese food. Father saw it and laughed, then said,

"Luke, you need to realize that each nation has their own favorite food, and if you are invited to eat, you must at least have the good manners to eat their food."

I smiled and nodded, but I was wondering what the food would be like. The coolies that worked on the railroad ate steamed rice with just a few pieces of dried fish on the rice. Yes, I could eat their food, maybe just once.

Decorated with many dragons, symbols and writings, the Chinese restaurant, had some rather odd sounding, twanging music playing in the background. I could see the musician, sitting on a pillow, playing a long stringed instrument in his lap.

When we sat down, I noted the lack of silverware, and the two sticks in a folder. I looked at my Father and his host, who both began to laugh. I was somewhat relieved when a waiter brought each of us an odd-looking spoon and a fork.

Our guest ordered dinner, and my Father began to tell our host about what I had seen in the lobby of our hotel. He was upset and said,

"I know the owners of that hotel, and will make it a point to drop by and see them."

The remainder of the discussions that night were on the worth of some stocks, and what the projections were for its' increase in value. It was Greek to me, so I ignored all of it.

Actually, the Chinese food was not that bad. Yes, there were some odd tasting dishes, but with something called sweet and sour, I made it through, and had plenty to eat.

The next morning we began our journey back west. In the New York area, the trains seemingly ran right through towns, sometimes elevated and sometimes at ground level. It was late afternoon before any significant green grass or crops were visible. On occasion, the rails ran over, under and around larger cities, and factories. Then I went to sleep. We did not have sleepers for this first night, so I curled up on the floor in a blanket.

The first time we had to change trains, Father sent a telegram to Mrs. Scott. It provided the time when we would arrive in St. Louis, and that we would like to visit. And, if it was convenient for her, to please send a confirmation wire to a certain station.

The next day Father and I got off the train to stretch, and he checked for a telegram from Mrs. Scott. There was none.

I could tell that my Father was disappointed, but he said,

"I suppose our schedules did not match."

I challenged Father to a game of checkers, and was soundly trounced a couple of times. I then began to read one of the books Father had purchased in Boston. When I began to read my Father smiled broadly.

I asked,

"What?" He said,

"I was thinking of the many times that I reread a month old newspaper, just to have something to read." He then told me how that in the west, a single book was often traded to other people for another book. These books are passed around for years, and that often, books are traded and discussed, even on cattle drives.

I suppose these comments triggered Father's desire to read, and he told me of how he had once traded for a book, only to discover that he had already read that particular book. Some of the more popular books were on law and even Greek mythology.

He then, gave me a short lecture on reading. In addition, he made it a point to inform me that Abraham Lincoln had been teethed on the Bible. He also said,

"Often, you can tell if someone had read a particular book, by the words they use when they are speaking."

I knew that Father was constantly reading something, even when he should have been resting. I asked about that, and he said,

"Luke, it takes some special effort to put your ideas in order, and even more effort to write a book. I know that I can benefit by those people who have put that extra effort toward writing a book."

That got me thinking, and I sat quiet for a time, and said to Father,

"You should write a book." He looked at me, then, laughed.

Our discussion about the value of books made me think of that sailing ship book I read at the hotel in Boston. If I had not read that book, I would not have known that a sailing ship can sail into the wind.

I again I thought of the possibility of putting a large sail on a train. But, the western plains are rarely flat, and an enormously large sail would be required to go up hill. The more I thought of books, the more I appreciated what Father had said. Yes, some extra effort would be necessary to write a book.

We arrived in St. Louis almost on time, and when we got off the train, there at attention, stood Jenkins.

CHAPTER 14
TARGET SHOOT

Jenkins winked at me, and I felt much better. Then he said,

"Mrs. Scott has just returned from a visiting trip, and did not get your Telegram until today. She begs you and Luke to come and visit a few days."

My Father said,

"Thank you Jenkins. Could you see to the baggage while I take care of our tickets?"

Jenkins said, "With pleasure."

I went with Jenkins and a fellow with a red cap to the curb, and loaded our things into the carriage. It was getting late in the day, and turning cool, so I climbed into the carriage too. It was nice to be with friends again.

Later, Father came out of the terminal door, and immediately saw the carriage. As he jumped in, he said,

"Off we go Jenkins." The horses also seemed eager and hit a good stride. By the time we turned into the covered drive, I was asleep.

When I awoke, the first thing I saw was my Father, lying next to me, breathing easy, fast asleep. Again, we were in the blue room. I arose, washed my face and got dressed, and went directly to the banister. Even before I reached the bottom, William appeared, with a large smile.

He led the way to the kitchen, where I was welcomed by those two ladies. I gave them both a hug, which made their eyes misty as they turned to make breakfast. William disappeared, but I went to the small table and sat down, as a glass of milk was set before me.

Soon I was attacking a large plate of eggs, ham, and biscuits. Just as William was setting down, the swinging door opened, and there stood my Father. The ladies' giggled, as he spoke to them. Pouring himself a cup of coffee, he came and sat down, insisting that William join us.

Just as the ladies were bringing my Father's breakfast to the table in walked Mrs. Scott. I stood, as did my Father and William. She said,

"Sit and eat your breakfast, do you mind if I join you?"

Father held her chair, got her coffee, and said,

"My great thanks for your generous hospitality."

She said,

"Bill you know that you are always more than welcome in my home."

It was a cozy breakfast, with good conversation, and the best of food. Then, it dawned on me,

"I do not know anything about Mrs. Scott." I said as much, which caused everything to stop. My Father looked at her, and she at him, then she said,

"I suppose he is old enough to know."

Looking right at me, she said,

"Luke, once, out on the prairie, your Father saved my life. Actually he saved me and my husband's life, when we were attacked by some Indians." I looked at my Father.

Finally, he said,

"It was at a rail-head, we were pressing forward at a rapid pace. Moving so fast we were out pacing most of the rail building crew. Then, a small group of renegades attacked us. With some luck, I was able to stop their War

Chief and two others, which broke their attack. I had one of those rapid firing Winchesters and was able to keep them off us until more of our crew arrived."

He had never told me about that.

Mrs. Scott, said,

"What your Father said is true, but he only told you the basic facts. I feel sure, Luke, you can imagine what happened."

I looked at my Father, and then slowly nodded.

Mrs. Scott then said,

"That is enough about Indians." I looked at the two kitchen ladies, they were white as a sheet, and William was in a bit of shock.

Continuing, she said,

"Let's retire to the library where we can be more comfortable."

A library, in a house? This I have to see!

Across the large entryway hall, a set of double doors opened to yet another large room where two walls were nothing but shelves and shelves of bound books. Yes, it was a library, all right!

My Father and Mrs. Scott began talking of things, and I went to the shelves of books, reading the labels. There were many I had never heard of, but some that I had. A large world globe sat in one corner and I went to it. It was amazing to see how the landmasses are laid out, on the real shape of the earth. Longitude and Latitude lines covered the globe, and I quickly located St. Louis, and the Mississippi River. It dawned on me that my Father and Mrs. Scott had stopped talking, and were watching me examine the globe.

Awkwardly, I said,

"I have never seen such a globe before."

They both chuckled. Then Mrs. Scott said,

"There is a target shoot being held today, why don't we go as spectators? I jumped, and ran to Father, who looked at me for just a moment and said,

"Yes, why don't we?"

Mrs. Scott walked to the wall, pulled on a rope thing. Far away, I heard a 'ding' and shortly William came through the door.

She said,

"William, we are going to the target shoot today. Please arrange a lunch and the carriage. Oh, yes, I know that you will want to attend so you can change out of your uniform."

With emphasis, he said,

"Yes Ma'am!" and disappeared through the door.

It was a grand day. Two shooting clubs were competing for a trophy of some kind, but the thing I enjoyed most, was the opportunity to walk pass a very long table where the rifles were on display. I was a bit amazed at the depth of knowledge that my Father had about rifles and shooting. The long-range shootings that day were at 500 yards; so far, that it was even hard to see the target.

To my great surprise, William competed in one category, and finished third.

By the time, we returned to Mrs. Scott's home, I was pooped. A quick sandwich, and a glass of milk, and I was out of it.

I must have been extra tired, because the next morning when I came down Mrs. Scott and Father were already having breakfast on the back porch. Well, porch is probably not the correct description, but you get the idea. As I approached, Father was telling Mrs. Scott about the train wreck, and about my helping passengers out of the dining car. When he got to the part where the car caught fire and burned, she was shocked. However, she asked several questions.

While I ate breakfast, Father told of our trip to New York City and the apparent criminal activity that I had seen.

Then, Mrs. Scott said,

"Woops," Jumped up and left the porch. Shortly she returned with a newspaper, and pointed to a front-page article.

In sum, it told of a hotel that was catering to theft, and other criminal activities. The arrests were said to have been initiate by a recent guest, who had observed some of the criminal activity.

Father looked at me for a moment, then, winked, and we all had a laugh. Then Mrs. Scott asked where my Father was off to next. I paid attention, because I knew I would be going also.

After a short hesitation, he said.

"The Union Pacific is having some difficulties with their tracks coming across the Rocky Mountains, and has asked for my advice."

Mrs. Scott asked,

"Then, you will travel to the rail head, Denver, and farther west. Then perhaps even on by horseback?" My Father nodded yes. I did not eagerly seek another long train ride, but the horseback part sounded adventurous.

The next day we boarded a train for points west. Traveling across Missouri was not bad, because there were many, farms, fields of crops and many trees. Once we crossed the Missouri River, the scene changed drastically. There were few trees, lots of grasses, and often wheat fields to the horizon. The scenery was just flat boring, so I got into the book my Father had purchased.

Often, my readings were interrupted, as railroaders would drop by to discuss things with my Father. I learned that people eagerly sought Father's opinion on anything having to do with the railroads.

CHAPTER 15
ANOTHER TRAIN ROBBERY

One day, while we were waiting for a train in Kansas, a Mr. Fred Harvey came to see Father. He was planning a bunch of restaurants that would be in Depots, to feed the traveling public. I listened in, since the main topic was food. He was trying to come up with a plan to staff these places with women; he had tried men, but they all left to become cowboys.

My Father said,

"Just advertise in the eastern papers for single women to work in the west." Mr. Harvey was not sure that he could get sufficient help using that method.

Father said,

"Just you tell them the job will be in the west, and they will flock to you just for the excitement and unknown. However, you will need to keep those women strictly away from men, or they will get married. Women are in short supply west of St. Jo."

Then thinking a moment he continued,

"A good approach would be to have dormitories, with strict rules, and an iron-clad contract for say, for two years."

I thought such restaurants would do well in the west, because the food served by places that operated near Railroad Stations, was not so good. Just then, we pulled into a small Depot, and visited a rambled down shack that served bad food. I mentioned this to Father, asking, how they could remain in business. He said,

"They have a monopoly, and know it."

"What is a monopoly?"

"They have no competition."

I thought about that for a while, and asked,

"Will Mr. Harvey do that too?"

My Father laughed, and said,

"Yes, but he will run the others out of business, because he will offer superior food and service."

I said,

"I wish he were here now!" Father laughed.

The plains of Nebraska and Colorado as always provided boring scenery from a slow moving train. Occasionally, we would see cowboys, horses, a few buffalos and cattle, and even a stagecoach, but mostly it was just miles and miles of long stemmed grass and wheat.

There is something lonesome about the long grasses and wheat bending with the wind. We saw far fewer Buffalo than our last trip. The rail bed had been improved, and the clickity-clack from the rail joints was not so loud. Even though the countryside is mostly flat, occasionally the land would simply fall away, providing a vast scene. There could have been an entire army in that vista, and a passer-by would never have seen it.

At one watering stop, my Father and I got off to stretch and walk around. I did not see anything, but when the train resumed its trip, Father went to find the Conductor. Later, I noted that a couple of men had acquired rifles, and one sat in the first seat in each end of our car.

Father pulled me to him and said,

"Luke, if you hear anything out of the ordinary, I want you to hit the floor. Do you understand?" I nodded. I wanted to ask a question, but I was signaled to keep quiet.

As our train's engine began to labor, I noticed that the riflemen changed their sitting position, getting ready. However, soon the engine's speed picked up, and everyone relaxed.

My Father said,

"Back at that water tank, I saw someone using a glass looking at our train. I knew we soon had a grade to climb, and thought a robbery may be about to happen. I relayed this to the Conductor and he recruited a couple of fellows to stand by. Evidently, they did not have this train in mind."

So, I asked,

"Will the next train be robbed?" Father looked off across the prairie and said,

"I wonder." Then he got up and went to find the Conductor.

When he came back to our seat, he said,

"They are going to stop for a few minutes at the next telegraph station, and send a wire back down the tracks, alerting other trains of a possible robbery."

I was more than a little excited, and began to imagine all sorts of things. The train slowed as it came up a slight grade, and I heard a thump, thump, from the ceiling of our car. No one else seemed to notice, but my Father did. He looked at me and pointed to the floor. The door at the end of our car banged open, and a fellow stood in the door with a pistol in his hand, then, 'Boom!'

My ears were ringing. Looking up I could see that Father had a smoking pistol in his hand.

Looking under the benches, I could see a fellow sprawled out on the floor. The door at the other end of the car banged open, and my Father wheeled around, but saw that it was the Conductor with a rifle in his hands.

The Conductor ran the length of the car, stepped over the fellow on the floor, and went through the door and disappeared. Then 'Boom, Boom' we heard him shoot. This was the second time I had witnessed an attempted train robbery. Both had failed. I wondered why outlaws thought they could rob a train. When I said this to Father, he reminded me, that several gangs had successfully robbed trains. Gangs like the James brothers, and the hole-in-the-wall gang.

I thought, maybe I have just been lucky.

Chapter 16
A Detective

At the next water tank, we disgorged the former outlaw, and Father sent a telegram back down the rail line. He described the attempted robbery and warned other following trains to be prepared.

Discovering that there were no lawmen anywhere nearby, the body was re-loaded into the Express car, to be transported to the next town. It turned out to be Denver.

My Father and I spent a good two hours answering questions about the attempted robbery. Finally, we were allowed to go to a hotel for the night. The next day, my Father told me that with the increase in lawlessness, he had decided to locate a place I could stay while he completed his assignment for the railroad. I protested, but Father had made up his mind, and I knew he would not change it.

I remained in and around the hotel most of the day, watching the people and traffic. Things must have been booming, because the roads were very busy. From the window in our room I could see the railroad depot, and watched the trains arrive and depart. I counted three different railroads servicing Denver.

I was getting bored watching people and things, when I saw a well-dressed man get off an incoming train. Two rather weary looking riders met him. They were such ill-matched individuals, that I could not help but think that something was amiss. The fellow, who came in on the train, carrying a valise, came walking toward the hotel. Quickly, I descended to the lobby, and sat in a stuffed chair.

He came through the front door, went directly to the desk, asked for a room. When he was signing the register, I noted the initials of "H. H. K." imprinted on his valise. He then went upstairs. While the desk clerk was not looking I peeked at his signature, it was, "C. Dennis."

Ah Ha, I thought. He is either traveling with someone else's valise, or he is incognito. I hung around the lobby for more than an hour, but I did not see him again. While I was sitting there in the lobby, I practiced my observation techniques Father had taught me.

He had said,

"Almost everyone has a mannerism, flaw, or scar that makes him unique." I decided that I would try to identify this fellow's unique identifier, and then see if Father could see the same thing.

Father soon came back to the hotel, saying,

"The family I had in mind for you to stay with while I am away is out of town, and will not return until sometime tomorrow." When he asked what I had been doing all day, I told him of the fellow I had watched. He asked if I had noticed anything peculiar to his person. I said no, but I had only seen him once. Out of the corner of my eye I saw the valise that fellow had been carrying. I whispered this to Father.

He arose, and walked toward the coffee pot, filed his cup, and returned to our table. Sipping his coffee, he leaned over and whispered to me, "Describe the fellow that you saw earlier today." I did.

Then he looked at me with a puzzled face, and grinned. Then Father said, aloud,

"Let's go out on the porch for some air." On the porch, he moved to a position where we could see the fellow with the valise through a window. Then he said,

"Luke, I think that is the same fellow, but he is wearing a disguise."

I turned and looked, looked close.

"Maybe," I said, "But he is heftier than before." Father said,

"That is easy to change with a pillow."

From behind us, someone said, "Hello Bill." I about jumped out of my skin. It was Marshall Cook. He shook our hands, and asked if we were going to be in town long. Father told him about him trying to find a family I could stay with while he completed some railroad work. Then Marshall Cook said,

"Heck, Bill he can stay with us. We would be glad to have some company."

So a deal was struck, for the next month or so I would stay with the Marshall's family. As we stood there and talked, Father pointed to the fellow with the valise; and pointed out that he appeared to be wearing some sort of a disguise. After a long look by the Marshall, he said,

"I do not recognize him, but I will make it a point to keep tabs on him."

The next morning we carried my bag to the Cook's home, we were introduced around, and I was assigned a place to bed down. My Father tried to pay for my keep, but the Marshall and his wife would not hear of it. The Marshall's son, Ken, was about my age, and we got along swimmingly.

The next morning at breakfast, Marshall Cook, looked at me and Ken and said,

"I have a job for you two boys today."

We both ducked our heads wondering what menial labor task he had in mind. He said,

"Luke, you know that fellow at the hotel who appears to be in disguise? I want you two to keep tabs on him. I want to know where he goes, who the talks to, and if he wears more than one disguise. Additionally, I want to know the time every event occurs. Can you do that?" I looked at Ken, and we both said, in unison,

"Yes sir."

He continued,

"Most people pay little attention to youngsters, but if this fellow is up to no good, he will be especially vigilant, so you will need to be seen as little as possible." We nodded.

"Ok then. I have arranged with the hotel that for the next few of days, one of you will be their runner; to deliver messages, and take or bring horses to and from the Livery. Watch carefully, and try not to make him suspect that he is being watched. If there is even a slight chance, he has noticed one of you, switch places. And if you need to see me to report something, use the rear door of my office."

Ken and I sat on the Marshall's front steps and developed some hand signals to be used if we needed to switch places.

I said,

"Hey, I feel like we are Deputy-deputy Marshall's." Ken laughed, and said that he had watched people before for his Dad, and it is mostly just boring work. With that, we walked toward the hotel, and flipped a coin to select who was to be the errand runner first. I won.

I went directly to the Desk Clerk, and introduced my self, and he said,

"Just stay out of the way, until I call you."

I found a chair in a far corner of the lobby, and settled in for a long wait. I had hardly sat down when that fellow came down the stairs. I had a good view of him, and noted that he favored his left leg. It was a very slight limp. It was not likely to be noticed, unless you were looking close. He nodded at the Desk Clerk, and went out the front door of the Hotel. I moved to a window, signaled Ken, who pointed at the fellow, and I nodded.

I watched as Ken dogged the fellow walking down the street, then, I heard the clerk calling my name. I went to the Desk, and was told to go to the Livery, and bring Mr. X's (I forget his name) horse to the hotel. I ran down to the Livery, and told the proprietor that I had been sent to bring Mr. X's horse to the hotel.

While he was saddling the horse, I walked to the street looking for Ken. Finally, I located him, sitting on a step of a store whittling on a stick. He nodded is head, indicating that our fellow was in the bank. I looked at the clock in the church steeple.

When the horse was ready, I lead it back toward the hotel, making it a point to go near Ken, who whispered, that he had been in the bank for some time.

I said, "Go in and get change for your half dollar." (Marshall Cook had given us each a half dollar as pocket money for our task.) I continued on to the hotel, tied the horse at the hitch rail, and went in and reported in to the Desk Clerk.

Inside the lobby, I moved to a chair that provided a view, of the street. I had just settled in when the Desk Clerk waved to me. He wanted me to sit on the hotel porch, and save the lobby chairs for boarders.

I was out on the porch for about an hour, when I saw our fellow coming up the street. I got up and walked around the far side of the hotel, and peeked around its corner. Our subject, went right in, climbed the stairs, and disappeared from view.

Ken came to my position, and said that our fellow had been talking to an officer of the bank, a Mr. Gilliland, who sat at a desk behind the railing. He also said that this bank officer seemed to be very nervous.

To Ken I pointed out that the fellow seemed to be favoring one leg. Ken said,

"Yes, his left leg." Just as we were running out of things to discuss, the fellow came out of the Hotel, and headed down the street. Ken followed at a distance.

In just a few minutes Ken came running toward me, panting he said,

"He is renting a horse at the Livery."

I said follow me, we went up the back stairs of the Hotel, and sat on the top step. Soon, he came riding by, crossed the railroad tracks, heading south.

We watched him as he became smaller and smaller, just before he passed from our view, two riders joined him.

Ken and I discussed whether we should report what we had seen. We decided that we had nothing of substance to report. I returned to the Hotel porch, and Ken wanted to check in with his Father, and went to find him.

Chapter 17
Bank Robbery

I was bored! Ken was off hunting his Father, and I was stuck at the hotel playing nursemaid to horses. I had made two trips to the livery, and all I got out of them was a nickel tip. It was approaching lunchtime; my stomach had announced that fact. My nose had discovered an aroma emanating from an unseen, unknown location that was up-wind of the hotel. I had to sit on the far side of the hotel porch, to keep the aroma from flooding my nose.

I suppose this distraction caused me to relax my vigilance, and I almost did not see our fellow until he had passed the hotel. I scanned the street, looking for Ken, but did not see him. I thought about going to the Livery so I could trail our man, but then thought I had better stay at my agreed position. Time seemed to pass very slow.

Just as I was trying to think of an excuse to go to the livery, I saw our man coming down the street. Glancing at his progress every now and then, I saw Ken dogging his heels. The next time I looked down the street, he had disappeared. I could not see Ken either. I stood up, walked all around the porch, but could not locate him. Then, Ken's head appeared around the corner of a building, and he nodded toward that store, indicating that he was inside.

Taking a risk, I left the hotel porch to look at the church clock, and to take a peak at the store our target had gone into. It was a restaurant.

Now my saliva glands began to squirt fluid. My stomach rolled and I had visions of potatoes, gravy, and biscuits. My stomach did another flip-flop. It was pure torture!

I heard the Desk Clerk call me, and reluctantly I turned around and entered the lobby. There was no one at the desk, so I began to wonder what was going on. As I walked up to the desk, the clerk said,

"If you will go to the kitchen, they will provide you a sandwich for your lunch."

Quick as a wink, I was in the kitchen, admiring their fixings. The lady cook, saw me standing there, and motioned me over to her. She commenced to carve a thick slice of meat, and placed it between two slices of bread. I was mesmerized, and just stood there. She asked, "Can you eat two sandwiches? I nodded yes.

She wrapped the sandwiches in paper, handed them to me, and said,

"Now, get out of here." I slipped out the back door, signaled to Ken. He came on the run. We climbed the hotel's outside stairs and stuffed our selves with the food. As we ate, I asked Ken if the rooms in the hotel had locks on the doors.

He asked

"Why?" I said,

"I was wondering if we could get a look in that fellow's room." He thought on that, and we decided that the next time he left the hotel, I would see if I could discover his' room number, and try the door.

Finishing our lunch, I went back to the porch and Ken took a position across the road, leaned on a hitch rail, and began to whittle on a stick. Just a couple of minutes before two o'clock, by the church's clock, our target came down the front porch steps and went up the street toward the bank.

I watched as he, and then Ken, cross the street, and disappear in the traffic. Then I turned and went to the hotel desk, I had decided that I would ask for the guests room number. I was going to use the excuse that the man at the livery wanted to know, but the clerk just spun the registration book around, and said,

"Read for your self."

The entry read, C. Dennis, then, room 233. I said thanks, and went back to my porch position. It was a boring afternoon, except when three cute girls came bouncing along the street. I watched them until they disappeared. I think they liked being 'looked at'. We had not spoken about how long we would stay at our posts, but when the sun began to go down, I wished that I had brought my jacket.

I vowed that if we did this tomorrow, I was going to insist that we change positions. Then I remembered that I was to try to have a look in his hotel room. Wandering around in the lobby, I sneaked up the stairs when the desk clerk was distracted. The door to his' room was locked! I thought about trying to jimmy the lock, but then thought that might get us into big trouble. I wondered what I may have missed in my first assessment of this fellow in a disguise.

As dusk began to settle, the temperature began to drop rapidly, and now I really wanted my jacket. Just as I was about to call it quits, I saw Ken coming up on the far side of the street. Our target also appeared. He went into the lobby, and directly into the restaurant. I was glad he did, because I could now sit inside. Looking up, Ken and the Marshall came to the hotel door, and motioned for me, to come outside.

Marshall Cook had my jacket under his arm, which I quickly donned. He then said,

"Ken has given me a rundown on our interesting fellow, do you have anything to add

"Not much. I tried his room door, and it was locked." Then, he just stood there thinking.

Then he said,

"Well, there is really no indication of foul play, so I think we had better head home for supper." Boy that sounded good.

At the supper table, we had to repeat our discoveries to Mrs. Cook. Who, seemed to be thinking, as were we. Then, she asked,

"You say that the fellow hung around the hardware store all afternoon?"

Ken said, "Yes Ma'am."

"Isn't that just across the street from the bank?"

The Marshall's head jumped a foot.

CHAPTER 18
NITROGLYCERIN

The Marshall said,

"I had forgotten that fact." He got up, went to get his hat and gun belt, put it on, and said,

"Ken you and Luke run down the street and tell my deputy to come a running to the bank."

I followed Ken as he ran out the door. The deputy was sitting at super when we banged through his front door. Ken, repeated what the Marshall had said, and even before the tale was finished, he was belting on his gun. I looked at his wife, and was surprised to see real concern in her face. Here, Ken and I were behaving as if it was just a wild adventure, but she was really worried.

Striding swiftly the Deputy went through the front door, with Ken and I, right on his heels. Just as we reached the road and turned toward the center of town, we heard BOOOM! And a big fireball rose in the sky! The flash was like a monster lightening strike right in front of us.

The deputy and the two of us were now running at top speed. As we closed on the bank there were several people standing around staring. Marshal Cook was announcing for everyone to stand back off the street. All I could see was a tangled mess of stuff all around the front of the bank. I did note that the windows of the bank were all busted out. Marshal Cook handed his keys to Ken and said,

"Run to my office, and bring me that large paper pad on my desk." Turning to me, and his' deputy, he said,

"You two keep the people back so they will not destroy any evidence."

I heard someone running fast, and he was coming right at me. I quickly got down on all fours and knocked his feet out from under him, and he went sprawling in the street. That attracted the Marshall. He helped the fellow to his feet, and before the fellow could speak said,

"Yes, Mr. Gilliland I know it is your bank. Nothing inside is amiss, I need you to help us (he waved his hand at the deputy and me) keep the people back from this debris, which is evidence, or we may never know what happened here."

The banker stood shocked still, looked around, and said,

"Right," and began to help us keep the crowd back. Ken came running to the Marshall and handed him a large pad of paper.

Looking at me, then at Ken, he asked,

"Which one of you is the best artist?" We shrugged our shoulders.

"Ok, you two decide. Here is what I want you to do. I want a complete to-scale drawing of every object or piece laying here in front of the bank."

"You can mark the spot where each item is found with a number. Then make a list of what each number is, and how much it weighs. Have you got that?" Ken nodded, but asked,

"How do we decide how much each item weighs?"

Turning to Mr. Gilliland the Banker, he asked, "Could you help with identifying each Item and its' weight?"

"Sure. But may I make a suggestion?"

The Marshall nodded.

"Marshall, there are some human body parts in this mess. I recommend that you have someone obtain some blankets and cover them. Then, we can try to discover who they were later."

"Good idea. Ken, run and get the doctor, if he isn't here already, and also get the undertaker."

Then, the banker and I, with the help of the Marshall and his deputy cataloged every item we could find. Once I picked up a boot, to guess its' weight, but it was too heavy for a boot. When I looked inside of the boot, it had a severed foot in it!

I immediately dropped the boot.

The banker asked, "What is it?"

I just pointed at the boot. When he picked the boot up and looked inside, he set it back down very carefully.

Finally, we had all of the body parts, and other stuff we could identify and marked on the paper. Then the Marshall had us go inside the bank and do the same thing. However, most of the items in the bank were glass fragments from the windows and a bunch of papers scattered all around.

The Marshall told the deputy to take me to the hotel, and see if our suspect was still there. As we approached the hotel, we could see the Desk Clerk on the porch. The deputy turned to me, and said,

"You ask."

CHAPTER 19
SEARCH FOR ATTEMPTED BANK ROBBERS

I asked,

"Is Mr. C. Dennis still here?" The Clerk stood startled, and then said,

"No. He checked out about two hours ago."

I said to the deputy,

"Do you think we should look in his room?"

He said,

"Good idea."

Nodding, the Desk Clerk followed us up stairs, and unlocked the door, and then the deputy said to the clerk,

"You had better wait here in the hall."

There was nothing in the room but a small box that was left sitting next to the water bowl and pitcher. The deputy opened the box, and scanned its contents, and a question in his voice asked,

"What is this?"

Looking over his' shoulder, I said,

"It is an actor's makeup kit."

We took it back to the Marshall's office. The Banker, Ken and the Marshall were studying papers hanging on the wall. It was drawings of the debris patterns from the road and inside the bank. Then the doctor came into the office.

The Marshall looked at the doctor and said, "Well?"

The doctor said,

"My first guess is that there were the remains of just one person and one horse in front of the bank."

The Marshal then said,

"I have information that makes me believe that there were three men involved in this aborted bank robbery. Does anyone have information on the other two?"

No body spoke.

Then he turned to the Banker and said,

"I also believe that one of the three, possibly the one blown up, entered your bank yesterday, and personally spoke with you."

I thought the Banker was going to faint. He had to sit down. After a few minutes he asked,

"Are you sure?" The Marshall nodded.

I heard a swish, swish behind me and turned around to discover someone was taking notes; probably a reporter. I cleared my throat, which caused the Marshall to look at me. I nodded my head toward the reporter.

The marshal addressed the reporter, and said,

"I want to read what you are going to print before you go to press. There are at least two more robbers out there somewhere, and we do not want to frighten them away.

The reporter nodded an ok.

Turning back to the Banker, he said,

"I need you to describe the people that you spoke with yesterday; the people that you do not personally know."

However, the banker knew much less than Ken and I.

The Marshall then turned and said,

"Do we have a mining engineer with us?" No one spoke up.

He looked at Ken, who ran out the door. In just a couple of minutes, he came back with a fellow in tow.

The Marshall quickly reviewed what he knew, what he suspected, and showed the debris pattern sketched on the hanging paper. Then, asked,

"What do you think caused the explosion?"

He studied the paper for a couple of minutes, and said, "Nitroglycerin."

The Marshal asked, "How so?"

The miner then described how sensitive the stuff is, how easy it is to set it off, and concluded with,

"If who ever were carrying the Nitro, even tripped or stumbled, that could have set it off."

.

Chapter 20
Catching Bad Men

I think we got to bed about four in the morning, but the Marshall was still sending telegrams to Sheriffs, and other lawmen in the immediate area. I slept late. When I awoke, the house smelled of food, and that awakened my stomach. After washing, I went into the kitchen, and Mrs. Cook was baking something that made my stomach do a flip-flop.

She opened a stove door and put some biscuits and bacon on a plate, for which I was very grateful. I did not see Ken, so I asked about him. He had been awakened by his' Dad, and was currently at his office.

Quickly, I made short work of the biscuits and bacon, and announced that I too was going to the Marshall's office. Mrs. Cook just smiled and nodded.

I arrived just in time to see that a posse had been formed, and was about to leave town. Ken was coming down the street, carrying some telegrams, which he handed to his' Dad. After reading each telegram, he handed them to Ken. Then he said,

"My deputy will take half of you fellows and head south. One of these telegrams describes a stranger camped about ten miles south."

"The other half will go with me. I have no other information to go on, but I feel that they may have headed west into the mountains, where there are few telegraphs."

"Remember, you are deputized US Marshall's and represent the law. If we can catch them, we will need them both back alive, to discover what really happened."

They rode off down the main street. There were many people there to see them depart. I turned to Ken, and he said,

"You and I are to man the US Marshals office. We are to read incoming telegrams, and answer those that need answering." I smiled!

Wow! We were right in the middle of a big robbery event.

Throughout the day, people dropped by, wanting to know what was going on. To keep from answering the same questions, repeatedly, we obtained the Marshall's approved Newspaper story, and hung it on a wall so people could read it themselves. Even so, we were still bombarded with many questions. Some did not make sense, but we tried. I could see that some people were making up stories, and just wanted to get us to validate them.

By dark, the visits to the office were dwindling, but the telegrams were peaking. It kept one of us going to the telegrapher almost constantly. As advised, we did not answer a telegram unless it was necessary.

Later, I wondered if they knew that a couple of twelve and thirteen year olds were holding down a U.S. Marshall's office.

The posses' returned after dark, neither found any thing, or anyone involved in the Bank blast. Marshall Cook and his deputy took over, and Ken and I retired to supper and a good night's sleep.

At breakfast, the next morning, Marshall Cook spoke to us about the recent events. First, he thanked us for our good work, and admitted that he had asked us to watch that suspect, mostly just to keep us busy. He apologized. Then said,

"I have insisted that your names be left out of the news stories, primarily to keep you from getting the big-head, and to keep you from being constantly pestered with questions."

"In a week or so, when things settle down, maybe I will let our local newspaper reporter print his embellished version."

Then,

"I don't suppose that you would be interested in another assignment?" Ken and I looked at each other and vigorously nodded affirmative.

"When you have caught-up on your neglected chores, come on down to my office." Those chores got done in record time, and we were on our way.

CHAPTER 21
WANTED OUTLAWS

Next morning at the U.S. Marshall's Office, the Marshall seated us at a small table, and we were given a stack of Wanted Posters. The Marshall said,

"Denver is right on the edge of the frontier, and every bad guy that has a reward on him wants to hide-out in the mountains to the west."

"With the railroad now in Denver, many of the 'wanted' pass through Denver to hide, plan or be involved in some criminal activity. I want you two to study these posters, until you can recognize each one. Then, I want the two of you to work around the railroad trains, and see if you can identify some of them. You are not to become involved. Should you 'think' you have seen one of those fellows on a poster, you hot-foot it back here and let me know."

We knew he was serious, and understood what we were to do. After some discussion he continued,

"Many outlaws wear some type of disguise, so try to picture the clean shaven ones with whiskers, and visa versa."

"Some of these fellows will try to leave a train before it reaches a town. It may be that you can have better luck at a position about a mile from town. I will let you decide when you would like to try that, and I will get you a horse to go to and from your selected site. I caution you that you will need an excuse for being out there. But, well, you just think on it."

"Study the posters today, and start tomorrow. You may find it helpful to pick up railroad schedules sometime today."

As I lay in bed that night, I wondered what Mrs. Scott would say if she knew Ken and I were hunting wanted outlaws?

Like most new activities, the first few days on this lookout assignment were exciting, however, the excitement faded fast. It seemed to us, that all of the outlaws had retired! It was almost two weeks before we had our first sighting. For a cover, we were washing the windows of the Depot for 10 cents for each of us, when Ken thought he saw a match to a poster.

I did not think it was a good match, but followed his lead. The fellow was carrying a saddle when he got off the train, and he carried it to the Livery. Many cowboys slept in the livery, when they had no money.

We hurried to the Marshall's Office and ran through the Wanted Posters again. Ken found the one he thought it was, and after looking at it for some time, I too thought it might be him. We told the Marshall where we saw him last, and he and his deputy headed for the livery.

Anxiously we waited in the Marshall's Office. Time sure passes slow when an anxious moment is at hand. Wondering what the penalty was for false arrest, both Ken and I looked at that wanted poster until it was burnt into my brain. I think I must have gone to the door and looked down the street ten times. Ken only looked five times.

Then we heard spurs jingling as someone approached. In came the deputy, followed by the fellow we had identified, and then the Marshall. The fellow was in handcuffs, and was put into a jail cell. The Marshall signaled with his head for us to follow him out side.

There he said,

"I think this may be him, but I can't be certain. I will have to send a telegram to the agency that posted the reward to know for sure. In any case you have done well and I congratulate both of you. You can now get back on the job."

We went back to finish the window washing, and received a lengthy berating for abandoning our job. The Depot agent muttered over and over that modern children had absolutely no sense of responsibility. We apologized, and went back to work. The remainder of the afternoon, we discussed and talked about the possibilities of having identified a bad man, but came to no conclusions.

The next day, we walked east down the railroad tracks about a mile, looking for a place where people might get off the train. While we were there, a train came from Denver. Headed east, it passed us. Watching it go away, we saw a fellow run from the brush, and jump on the train. We looked at each other, and laughed.

We decided to go to that spot and see what that place was like, and see how hard it would be to 'Catch a Train.' To our amazement, there was trampled down grass that indicated that this place had been used over and over, as a place to get on and off trains.

Back at the Marshall's Office, we told about what we had discovered. The Marshall said,

"Yes, I know the place you discovered. There are many down and out fellows, just trying to get home, who ride the rails. It would be a good place to watch, but you could be in some danger. Some of those fellows are dangerous. I do not want you to be around that place for any amount of time."

About then the deputy came in with some telegrams and mail. Opening one telegram, the Marshall showed it to his deputy. Then they went to the cell, and had the prisoner bare his left arm. The Marshall said, Ah Ha, and came to us and said,

"He is the one. He has a scar on his left shoulder that positively identifies him."

The Marshall shook our hands, and slapped us on the back, then took us to a saloon for a sarsaparilla. Boy did that turn us on. We got down all of the new wanted posters and began reviewing them, the Marshall and his deputy giggled.

Chapter 22
On the Lonesome Prairie

I suppose Ken and I thought that we would become the great duo of all time for catching wanted outlaws, but it was not to be. Our next two catches were wrong, and caused some disappointments in the US Marshall's ranks. The end being, we were retired as outlaw chasers at the Denver railroad Depot. However, that was not the end of our career.

Some months later Ken and I received a reward of $100 for the first bad man we identified. Fifty dollars each was big money for fellows our age. However, my Father and I were some distance from Denver when the reward money finally caught up with us. I wondered if Ken felt like I did, with big money burning holes in my pockets.

The money arrived at a good time. We were on our way to Cheyenne, Wyoming where the Union Pacific, had built their rail bed into Utah Territory. Father was telling me that the land rose significantly from western Nebraska to Cheyenne, and then went even higher before it rapidly dropped to the Great Salt Lake desert. Routing was therefore difficult, because the steam engines were running near their maximum puling capability.

The Union Pacific had actually reached Promontory Point in 1869, however many miles of the initial roadbed needed to be improved. This was especially true in places where the terrain rises sharply. Thus, Father was working with a crew of surveyors in examining better routes; routes that could easier be traversed by existing railroad engines.

He said,

"It is likely that more than one engine, or even specially designed engines may be required to pull heavy loads across the Continental Divide." That was the first time I had heard that term, and I asked for an explanation. He said,

"The Continental Divide is the point, actually it is a line, where rainfall on one side goes to the Gulf, and on the other side rain flows to the Pacific Ocean." I asked if you could see the line on the ground. He laughed and said,

"Not very often!"

My Father's work was in developing a rail bed that would allow a constant flow of rail traffic. To complicate matters the Indians were becoming more aggressive, some having acquired the newer repeating rifles. Soon we were moved back along the rail line to the east. This is where the climb to cross the Continental Divide really begins.

We slept, ate, and lived in a few rail cars on a siding. Two to three teams of surveyors were out every day exploring for possible alternative routes for a better rail bed. At night, they would all stand around a large table, on which a map was mounted, and discuss the day's progress.

Each night, the many dead ends discovered, were marked on the map. Now and then, another route would allow some progress, up to a point. The next day the survey teams would go to that new point, and try other courses. It was frustrating, but slowly progress was being made. Twice, Indians had appeared, and watched the surveyors drive stakes in the ground.

Many immigrant wagon trains had crossed this area, and even the Mormons had crossed with wagons and handcarts. However, a steam engine, pulling a string of heavy-laden rail cars, was another matter. For several months, I was practically confined to those rail cars, or their close vicinity. I saw great herds of Pronghorn Antelope, and some small herds of Buffalo, but that was about all.

I have to admit that it was interesting to meet some of the people going west. Almost everyone knew exactly where they were going, but had little information on how to get there. One day Father took me to a large rock formation, which seemed out of place. The rock was soft, and many travelers had stopped and carved their name in the rock. Even many well-known individuals had entered their name on the list of names.

Chapter 23
Rising Grade

For Almost a year, we worked that rising grade rail line. Several exciting things happened, but I will save that for another time. Always, looking for a better grade; a less steep grade. Sometimes father supervised a rebuild of a railroad bridge. But, often it was boring, boring. I really got tired of that rail coach that had become our home. Our exercise was hunting Pronghorn Antelope, upland game, and chasing long eared rabbits on horseback.

On rare occasions, a few people passed us on horseback. Most would stop, and pass the time of day, but they seemed to be on a mission, and hurried on. Then one day a long wagon train came inching by. I suppose they could not afford rail passage.

Those people traveling with that Wagon Train looked tired and worn out. Some seemed to be just putting one foot in front of the other. All asked,

"How far it was to someplace or another?" All I could tell them was that I did not know; it was an answer they did not like to hear. The creaking of the wheels of those large covered wagons left me with an eerie feeling. Most of these pioneers traveling by wagon were going up the Oregon Trail, where a rail line had not yet been completed.

One day when we were near Chimney Rock, Father took me on an outing to that tall edifice. You could see it from more than ten miles, and it seemed to get taller as we approached. Father and I had lunch near its' base, and I wanted to climb up to the level where the spire shot almost straight up. He did approve of a short climb up the sand stone bottom, and I can tell you, you could really see a long way. I could see the evidence of many others who had climbed.

I was exploring a sign carved into the rock when I heard the whine of a ricochet of a rifle bullet. I dropped flat on the rock, and listened intently for any sound. None, it was very quiet. In such circumstances, I had been taught to stay put for a long while, I only moved just a few inches off the rock so I would be lying in some sand. I listened and listened, but heard nothing. After a good hour of waiting, I crawled, slowly and as quiet as I possibly could to the edge, I looked down. Nothing, no one was in sight. Not even our horses.

My mind ran wild: as I thought of all of the bad things that could have happened. That passing, I knew that for some reason, my Father had left and took my horse with him. I remembered that he had always said,

"If we became separated, stay very close to where you were when we became separated."

It was mid-afternoon, and I thought that some pioneers might come by with some food (Not likely-now, most pioneers travel by train). Yes, that is just like me, thinking of food when my father might be in real danger.

After an hour or more, I became thirsty. I tried to remember if I had ever heard anyone talk about a source of water near Chimney Rock. I drew a blank. As the sun was getting down toward the horizon, I descended to the base of the structure. Looking close I discovered several empty cartridge cases, but none looked fresh. Horse tracks were everywhere, and I could make no sense of where they, who ever they were, had gone. Looking around, I spied a small green bush growing down to the north. Taking my time, I wandered in that direction. Zzzip! Something went by my ear.

I stopped to listen, just as I was taking another step, I heard it again. I remembered hearing people telling of following the flight of bees to water. I stood very still, and waited. Finally, a bee came right by me; it was heading toward that bush. Continuing down the hill, at the base of that bush I found a small seep.

It was actually just a wet place, with only a trickle of water. Cleaning the sand and dirt away, I made a small depression to catch and hold the water. Cupping my hands, I drank slowly. Then, I washed my face and hands. Soon it would be getting dark, and I knew that if I remained by the water, the animals would smell me, and stay away. I had to find a place to spend the night.

Not very far down the wash, I discovered where flowing water had cut under a bank. It was not much of a shelter, but I got my knife and cut several of the bushes nearby, and spread them on the ground. Limbs from other bushes, I broke off, and wove them together to form a crude blanket. Other tall limb's I used for covering the front of the bank cut. It was not cold, but I knew that the chill of night and the early morning dew, could really take the heat out of your body. I cut more dense brush and some reeds for bed padding. I knew I would not be able to sleep, but knew that I need the rest.

I was hungry, but knew I would have to tough it out. I took off my jacket, and laid it over my upper body, then covered the rest of me with the brush blanket and reeds. Not long after it got full dark, I heard animals coming down the wash to water. Some blew, and hesitated, but finally went to the water. Then it dawned on me,

"What had happened to my Father?" With that thought, I drifted off to sleep, and slept the night through.

Dawn woke me, and I was stiff and chilled. I gathered some dry sticks and built a fire. It is amazing how much a fire can do to raise one's confidence. When it was full daylight, I climbed out of the dry wash and had a good look around. I saw or heard nothing. I decided that I would climb back upon the monument's heights, that way I could see any one approaching. It was quiet. It was so quiet I could hear the blood rushing through my heart.

That afternoon it was a dry wind, which blew around the Chimney Rock. It increased in speed, and I saw some tumbleweeds rolling and bobbing along the ground. I was scared, but of what, I could not tell. Alone, is a good experience, it makes one appreciate his love ones.

It was late afternoon when I first detected a dust cloud on the horizon to the southeast. A wagon train? Indians? I squinted my eyes, trying to make it out. I was getting real hungry now and thought I should rig a snare or two to see if I could catch a Jackrabbit.

I descended to the brush along the wash, and found what appeared to be a well used game trail. I rigged a snare, by pulling a limb down on a large bush. Then I returned to my perch. What ever that was causing the dust, it was big, but they were to far away to tell what it was. We were well south of the railroad, so I never heard any train noises.

Finally I decided that the dust cloud must be from a herd of cattle, probably headed for Wyoming. However, at the rate they were traveling, I estimated that they would not get to my position for about two days. Nevertheless, just seeing that dust cloud, gave me a good feeling. I needed my snare to produce something to eat, but knew that it would be more effective at night. Before the sun was down low, I descended back down to the water seep. After a drink, I renewed my efforts at making a better bed and shelter, although there was not much else I could do.

Sometime during the night I was awakened by a fight going on in the brush, but they were not near, so I just turned over and went back to sleep. At daylight, I was up and had a fire going to get the chill off. Then I thought of my snare. I cautiously approached the snare, not wanting to scare any game away. I could see that the snare had been tripped, and hanging by its' neck was a large Jackrabbit. I skinned it quick, cut me a couple of green branched, and staked that rabbit over my fire.

I was hungry enough to eat that rabbit raw, but knew better. It began to smell oh so good. I was just about ready to cut me off a hind leg, when a voice said,

"I don't suppose you would be willing to share that breakfast?" It was Father! I ran into his arms and began to sob. A number of emotions went through my body. Anger that he left me. Wonder, why he left. Glad that he had returned, and proud, that I had survived. I asked about all of these questions and more, but Father said,

"Could we have breakfast before we talk?"

I believe that was the tastiest rabbit that I have ever eaten. It certainly hit the spot. Father then told me that some one had stolen our horses while we were rock climbing, and using his pistol he shot at the two culprits, and he had hit one of those fellows. He said,

"The one I had shot at fell out of the saddle, after he had ridden only a short distance. It was just a lucky shot with a pistol."

"Knowing that I had better get after the other rustler immediately, or there would be no likely hood of ever recovering our horses, I just began to run. I trailed the fellow and our horses into the night. Knowing that I could not approach the other horse stealer's fire, or the horses would give him away, I went on ahead of the rustler, and planned an ambush.

"At first light, I jumped the rustler as he rode by on a well defined trail. I ended-up having to shoot him too, and then waited for several hours as the rustler died. After a quick burial, I then began the return. Not knowing the situation here, I had waited until full daylight to approach, and was attracted by a good smelling breakfast."

I asked about the rustlers, but Father did not know who, what, or why they jumped us. I asked about the outlaw he had shot nearby, and he said that he had buried him this morning, but the night animals had already found him and were about to do their worst. Father gave me a real pat on the back for the way I had survived.

I told father of the dust cloud, that I thought was a heard of cattle going to Wyoming. After climbing upon Chimney Rock for a look, Father agreed that it was likely a heard of cattle. Father decided that we would ride toward the herd, and tell them of our rustlers. It was noon before we reached the lead rider (point man). He was a sun burnt fellow, skinny as a rail, riding a very strong horse, and he rode with a Winchester in his hands. He was surprised to see us, but invited us to share their evening meal. Pointing with his Winchester, he said,

"The chuck wagon will be set up along that creek."

A chuck wagon is a wonderful sight to see on the plains. The cook, a gruffly old fellow greeted us warmly, and said,

"The coffee will be ready in a few minutes." Ugh! It was very strong. I had to go to the water barrel and thin mine out before I could drink it. The cook was eager to hear of our recent adventure, and nodded when Father gave him a description of the two. He said,

"Those two shared our fire less than a week ago. Both fellows were offered drover jobs, but they refused. I do not believe those fellows wanted any kind of work.

Soon the cattle came near and many walked right into the shallow creek and drank. Several just stood in the water. The ramrod came in after the herd had circled and stopped for the night. He was a young fellow, but seemed to know his business. Around the campfire, Father retold of our adventures. It was not that unusual, but several glanced at me, wondering, I suppose, how a youngster would spend two nights alone on the prairie.

We remained with the herd for three days, working for our food, and I was getting the feel of a drover's job. In charge of the horse herd, about 40 strong, was a 12-year-old youngster. He was sun burnt so dark that his teeth seemed to glow in the dark when he smiled. That forth day, when the lead rider came into camp, he said,

"There are some railroad fellows up ahead. Said, they were looking for a man and a boy." Father laughed and said,

"A fellow just can not get away from the railroad." Everyone laughed; however they too knew how it felt to belong to a strong organization. Later two railroad detectives, Pinkerton agents, rode into camp. Some railroad big shot had sent them out to find us. This caused the drovers to take another look at father. He explained that he was working on a new rail route for heavy loaded trains.

Father spoke with the Ramrod and discussed the route they were taking into Wyoming. During the discussions Father said,

"In just a few years the rails will be available to ship cattle herds at fifteen miles and hour." This statement caused several of the drovers to squirm and realize that their jobs would soon be eliminated. I felt well accepted by the drovers. Some of them, there was about 15 drovers, were barely 15 or 16 years old. But, there was no doubt they did a man's work.

The Pinkerton agents escorted us back to our work train, and then left when the next eastbound freight train came through. I thought I could sleep for a week, but was up and around shortly after daylight. Father then interviewed me. He wanted to know every little thing I did and how I felt during the two nights I was alone. When he had finished asking questions, I felt much better, and my confidence soared.

It was often said, that we were right on the old Pony Express route, but they, had been replaced by the telegraph more than ten years ago. Of course, the trains passed each day, but they did not know that other routes were still being sought.

Every day we watched people that were moving west; one could see why the Indians were upset. Not only was their source of food been slaughtered, but even their life style was being swallowed up. Sometimes I would sit on top of our rail car and watch hawks and buzzards sailing in large circles, hunting for food. Then one day I had a visitor.

I was sitting right up on top of the railcar, when in the far distance I saw a lone rider approaching. This sight was not that unusual, but rarely did lone riders come by. He was coming directly at the rail car, and as he got closer, I could see that it was a small person.

Riding right up to the car, I could see that it was a young Indian. He sat there and looked the car and me, just as I was looking him over. After a while, he turned his attention to me, and spoke,

"I am Joseph."

I said, "I am Luke."

He sat there looking around, and I too examined him all over. The only weapon I could see was a knife in a waistband. He was wearing a buckskin shirt, a headband, with a feather; there were some symbols on the head band, moccasins, leggings, and a breach cloth of leather.

Then he spoke again,

"I see inside?"

I could not think of any reason to say no, so I nodded a yes. I climbed down, opened the end door to the rail-car closest to him, and stood by the door. He hopped off his horse, left the horse standing, and came up the steps.

I led the way down the crowded isle. He examined every item as we went down the aisle. He did not touch a thing. When he got to the place where we fixed our meals, he asked,

"Your Tepee?" I nodded a yes.

He seemed to be mesmerized by the big map on the table. He looked at it from every direction, then, he put his finger on the map, and said,

"Here."

He was right, that was right where the rail car was parked. He seemed like he had finished his survey, but he looked me in the eye and, asked,

"What do?"

I was at a loss for how to tell him what we were doing. But, I charged ahead. Pointing to the rail tracks on the map, I traced the rails. Then moved my fingers in a straight line, up over the rugged terrain, and said,

"Steam car no go."

He looked at me, then at the map. Looked back at me and, then he nodded, yes. Looking back at the map, he moved his fingers in a long arc to the north of the rails on the map, and said,

"More go."

He looked at my waist, then, I could see he was looking at the pistol in my belt. Now that I was older, Father had obtained a 38 revolver for me to carry when the crew was away from the coach. Then he looked at me for a long minute, then said,

"I go."

He walked out of the door, went to his horse, swung upon its back, and rode-off without a backward glance.

That evening I told my Father about my visitor. He re-cautioned me about letting anyone enter the car, but eventually had me tell him every little detail of the encounter.

He sat there a while, then, walked to the map, and said,

"Come show me where he drew his fingers on the map." I did.

He stood there a long time, then said,

"I wonder."

When the survey crews came in, he had me retell the map part of my encounter with the Indian. One of the crew said,

"Lets try that way, maybe there is something we have missed."

The next day the surveyors and Father came back all smiling. They had found a new route that would greatly ease the train's passage in that area. It was such a discovery, that we flagged down the next eastbound train, and our car was attached to the last car. It dropped our car on a side track at a place called North Platte. From there several telegrams were sent and received, from which, resulted in a new rail construction crew train heading west.

Father had been requested to come to Kansas City as soon as a new route was discovered. We took the next train going east. Reading an old newspaper I found on the train, it told about Jessie James robbing a train. I asked my Father why they had not caught that outlaw. He looked at me for a time, then said,

"He has been very difficult to catch, because he is revered in Missouri, and most of the people there tend to protect him."

I asked what revered meant. He explained, then, I said,

"But, he is robbing people and banks."

"Some people do not understand that it is really their money they are stealing. They have the notion that those people the outlaws rob have money that should belong to them."

I thought on that for a long while, then said,
"I hope this train isn't robbed."
Father smiled and said,
"Me too."
Kansas City was growing rapidly, with trolley cars, gas streetlights, and lots of people. The railroad Depot was very large; a person could get lost in that terminal. However, I was stuck in a hotel again, while Father went to another meeting. Beef seemed to be a big item in Kansas City. Restaurants specialized in select cuts of beef, and they drew large crowds each evening. Once, we went to one of those places, and I have to admit, they had good food.

However, the hotel was large, had shops in the lobby, and many more were near by. I sat and enjoyed watching the people come and go. Large changes had been made in Kansas City, but only people like Father and I really noticed. When you are close, and changes are made over time, I think it just looks normal. Often, I just got my nose in a book. Sometimes, I get lost in a book. If there is any unusual device or hint of adventure, in my mind I become the hero and visualize myself as the action person. When that happens, I shut out the rest of the world, like I am in a sort of a dream.

Then, I sensed that some one was staring at me. I looked up. It was Henry Long!

I jumped up and shook his hand, and he hugged me, and asked,
"Well Mr. Luke, what have you been up to?"
I told him about how Ken, the son of Marshall Cook, and I had received reward money, and how that came about.

Then I told him about the Indian who helped the surveying team find a better route into Cheyenne, Wyoming. He was very interested when I told of my being alone at Chimney Rock."
Henry said,

"My, you have been busy."

I asked what he had been doing. He said,

"Well I have been assigned to go to South America, to help them build a railroad down there."

Chapter 24
A New Adventure

I said that sounded exciting, and he laughed. Then said,

"I wonder if that is why your Father has come to Kansas City." Whoa! I did not like the sound of that, and said so. Henry laughed again.

I asked if he was available for dinner tonight, because I knew Father would want that. Henry said,

"It just so happens that I have tonight free." I was pleased.

As soon as Father came back to the hotel, I told him about Henry being here in Kansas City. And, that he had agreed to have dinner with us.

Father frowned, and said,

"Well I have been invited to a dinner to night, right here in this hotel. Maybe we can do both."

He went to the phone and spoke with the dining room, and made the necessary arrangements. Father, then told me to wear my best clothes to the dinner. This was a signal for a meeting with some big business men. Somehow, I didn't mind getting all suited-up, because there was always good conversation and food. I do have to admit, that there were very few boys my age at those fancy places. I remember the discussions after such meetings with Father; he treated them as educational events for me.

We arrived at the appointed hour, and were seated with an older couple; we had just sat down, when Henry arrived. Father explained that Henry was a long time friend of ours, and hoped that his 'dining with us would be ok. The Older couple was wealthy railroaders that both Henry and Father had known for years.

As is common with some businessmen, before dinner was even ordered, business was conducted. The older fellow, smiled and said,

"I suppose you have heard that Henry has agreed to go to South America to help us build a railroad there? My Father and I nodded. He then turned to Father and said,

"Bill, I also want you to go to South America. "

Father started to say no, but the older man quickly said,

"Just hear me out Bill."

"I know how you and your son work as a team, and we have received much information about your escapades both in the east and in the west. Nevertheless, I cannot feel comfortable with that effort down there in South America until you have examined the details of the job. I would like you and your son to go down there for just a month. Think of it, as the vacation that you never seem to have time to take."

I was flabbergasted. I could see that Father was more than a little startled. He turned to look at me, then turned back and said,

"My son and I will have to discuss this. We will let you know tomorrow."

That ended the business; and the meal ordered. However, you know, I do not remember what was served. All I could think of was South America; I was eager to get my hands on some maps.

Later that evening, I tried to get my Father to discuss the offer that was presented, but he said,

"I think we need to sleep on this decision, and give it some thought! Maybe we will have clear heads in the morning?"

We were in the hotel dining room shortly after 6 am. After ordering breakfast, Father asked,

"Well Luke, what to you think about going to South America?"

"It sounds like an exciting adventure, but I do not know very much about that place. I do understand that South America is very large, so I would guess that there will be large differences between the countries."

Father nodded, and said,

"Yes, and there are language differences; although, I am told that a person can get by if they speak Spanish."

Then for the first time my Father really took me into his confidences. He said,

"The only thing that makes me hesitate is the political situation. Railroads have been built in several countries in South America, but none of them has ever proved profitable or even somewhat successful. I have always prided my self in being able to finish an assignment, but somehow I feel uneasy about this one."

We just sat there for several minutes, not speaking, each of us in deep thought. Finally, Father said,

"I do not mind going to South America, but I need to make it clear that I will not be responsible for any failures that may occur."

With that, we finished breakfast, and headed for the railroad office.

CHAPTER 25
SOUTH AMERICA

On a bright sunny day we arrived in Rio de Janeiro aboard a freighter that had a few passenger cabins. My first time on the ocean was an experience. Neither I nor my Father had any seasickness, and the accommodations and food were acceptable. I was impressed with the large diesel engines that powered the boat. Father commented on their possible use in railroad engines, but there was no way to make a reliable connection to the drive wheels.

It was a sight, the beaches, the hills, and swarms of people, and Christos statue on that high mountain. Our accommodations were prearranged, and a 'Bigwig' of their local government, who was in charge of all railroading (he said), met us at the dock. This fellow was also very big in size, dressed in a rather flamboyant uniform, and with the usual face whiskers. Quickly he was trying to arrange a woman date for my Father. He seemed to assume that doing so would put him in a good position to leverage Father's favors.

After being rebuffed more than once, he changed tactics, and began hinting that for a small piece of the over all contract, he could make sure, that all necessary governmental approvals would be rapidly forthcoming. When my Father insisted that, the first thing he wanted to do was examine the overall plan of construction. Mr.

Big, (behind his back that is what Father and I called him) said that we would have to talk to his superior on any other matters.

He then gave us his telephone number, took his leave saying,

"I will be in touch soon."

Father winked at me, something he rarely did. He went to the telephone, and spoke with the operator,

"This is Mr. Markanis; I would like to speak with a Doctor Thomas Cochrane. He may be in the US or England, but please try to find him?"

"Yes, this is Mr. Markanis.

The Doctor's name, is spelled; COCHRANE.

Yes, that is correct.

Thank You."

Father turned to me and said,

"Doctor Cochrane is a very powerful person, and has constructed railroads in more than one South American country. He is a known figure in this country, and is almost feared by most high-level dignitaries in South America."

Father looked at his watch, looked at me and said,

"I bet the phone rings in less than five minutes."

The phone rang. My Father smiled, and said,

"I will wait for seven rings."

Answering after the seventh ring, he said,

"Hello."

"Yes, this is Mr. Markanis."

"Tomorrow morning at ten!"

"Yes, we will be waiting at the curb."

Then he laughed, and I joined in. He put his finger to his lips, indicating to be quiet, and, walked out on the balcony. I joined him. Father said,

"Every word of what we say will likely be heard. So, be careful of what and where you say something. Even when we are out and about, someone may be listening."

Luke, I want you to know that I may need you to give me assistance. I cannot say how or what, because I do not know what the situation may be. For example, if I feel we need to disengage a meeting, you could complain of a stomachache. Do you understand?"

I nodded my head, and he smiled.

Going back into our room, he said,

"Luke, would you like to walk around or what?

I said,

"I am pooped; I want to take a nap before supper."

Father said, "Good Idea."

That evening we dined on some very good seafood, that was served at a nice restaurant at an out-door table. After we ate, we just sat there and watched people that were out for a walk. Carriages were going too and fro, mingling in with trolleys pulled by horses, and at least one electric trolley.

I suppose I would be remiss if I did not mention the many dark eyed young ladies with tight fitting or sparse covering costumes that eyed Father. We went to bed early.

After some very good fruit for breakfast, we took a short walk, looking in shop windows and watching street vendors plying their trade. I was amazed at the number of two wheeled carts that patrolled the streets offering everything from fruits and nuts to meats of all kind. By 9:00 am we were getting dressed for the ten o'clock meeting.

The carriage that collected us at the hotel was nothing to shout about, but we only went a couple of miles. Arriving at a very large, white government type building, we were warmly welcomed at the door. During our escorted trip to a large upper room, I noted that things did not seem very orderly. Every building looked as if upkeep did not exist.

In the center of the room was a large table. On this table was a model of some terrain, with miniature railroad tracks winding through the sand box. It was then we discovered that traditionally, chocolate and coffee, were often served in this country. We refused both, and that seemed to raise some eyebrows.

I wandered around the room as the formalities were taken care of, then I sat in a chair by my Father. I took a clue from my Father, and kept my eyes away from the table and a large map on the wall. Eventually, everyone gathered around the table, as one fellow in a uniform, holding a long pointing stick, began to talk. Clearly, he was briefing my Father on the proposed rail line.

When he finished, my Father began to ask questions. He must have said 'why" two dozen times. One of the uniformed staff kept raising his eyes to the ceiling, when he knew my Father could not see him. Why, why, why, my Father kept seeking the reasons why the rail line was to take the proposed path. Why did it have to go through that valley, rather than a more direct route?

It was obvious that some of their staff were embarrassed by these questions. However, I noted a few nodded in approval when my Father asked a question. This went on until about one o'clock, when someone suggested that we break for the afternoon.

Father said,

"I know that I am not familiar with your customs, but my time here in your country is very limited. Therefore I would prefer that we continue with the discussions, until I have a full perspective of what is planned."

The Bigwig asked,

"What do you suggest?"

"I would suggest that light refreshments be brought in, and we stick with the presentation until we have covered all aspects of the proposed rail line. After that, I may have a few recommendations, and we can discuss those tomorrow."

"Of course, not everyone needs to remain here, just the members of the technical staff who have done the designing of the rail bed."

My Father had them by the neck, and they knew that if my Father did not recommend approval, the railroad would never be built.

So, it went until about midnight. People came and went, and another meal was brought in shortly after dark. Sometime after dark, I curled-up in a chair and went to sleep. Father woke me when the session broke up, and I heard Father say,

"I think we have made some progress, shall we meet again tomorrow at ten o'clock?"

At least half of the staff, pulled watches out of their pockets, looked at the time, then, looked at the ceiling.

The Big-wig had departed long ago, so his deputy, agreed. I went to sleep again in the carriage ride back to the hotel.

Chapter 26
A Bad Railroad Design

Father must have steered me up to bed, because that is where I awoke. He was shaving, and humming, when I walked up next to him and said, "How - - ?" Father looked at me, shook his head 'no', turned, and walked out on the balcony with soapsuds on his face.

I asked, "What did you think?"

"First you tell me what you observed."

I told him of some of the staff that kept looking at the ceiling when you asked questions,

"But, there were a few that often nodded approval when you were making a point. And, I think the Big-wig believes their project may be in big trouble."

Father looked at me and said,

"That is similar to my thoughts. The real trouble is that they have poor or no excuses for the route of the rails. Either I do not yet understand why, or it has been laid out to please land owners or the politicians, or both."

"When we get there to day, I want you to identify the staff members for me that were nodding in my favor. OK?"

"Are we going to stay until late again?"

"I hope not."

The carriage to pick us up was late. It was obvious that the driver had been told to take the long way around to our meeting. Father, leaned forward, and said something to the driver. The pace picked-up; we were only about 30 minutes late. A member of the staff met us at the curb, and escorted us to the big room. He seemed embarrassed that no one else had arrived, but Father ignored that and began to ask questions.

At first the staffer was reluctant to agree or disagree with Father's remarks, however he soon warmed to the subject, and they had their heads together in deep discussions. Soon another staffer arrived, and stood watching their discussions. Then something was said, that caused him to also get involved.

By the time the Bigwig arrived, there were several discussions in progress, with slide-rules zipping back and forth, and a large amount of notes being taken. Mr. Big just stood and watched for a few minutes, threw up his hands, and walked out of the room.

After lunch was brought in, Father, standing in front of the large map on the wall, got everyone's attention and said,

"I believe that I now have at least a working knowledge of the proposed layout of your railway. My major engineering concern is the proposed route."

"I have other engineering questions but they can not be addressed, until the route is finalized. I assume that you will want me to develop an alternate route, before we go any further?"

Dead silence. Mr. Big leaned over to his deputy and whispered. The deputy then rose and said,

"Mr. Markanis we greatly appreciate your efforts, but now we must have some time to discuss things within our staff before we proceed. Your carriage is waiting, and will convey you back to your hotel. We will contact you there soon."

I followed Father out and to the carriage. As we got going, I turned to say something to him, but he put a finger to my lips, and nodded toward the driver. I understood.

At the hotel Father said,

"I do not expect a call until tomorrow.

"How would you like to take a ride on the trolleys?" he asked. I nodded approval.

Changing our clothes, we stood in front of the hotel, and got aboard the first trolley that came by. It was a horse drawn unit, and it moved rather slowly through town.

I eagerly looked at the many homes and businesses as we rode in some comfort. Contrary to what I expected, this trolley riding, turned into a marathon. Father wanted to ride on them all! During our rides' I met, a fellow about my age named "Jose". He was the son of a trolley driver, and often rode just to be with his' Father. He was helpful in getting us on different systems, as he knew all of the routes and stops.

Later, while sitting at an outdoor café, I asked about our extended trolley ride. Looking around, Father said,

"I had heard that there were several trolley systems, using various modes of power, and operating on different types of tracks. Today, that was confirmed. They have three modes of power; horse, electric and steam, and, as many rail bed widths."

"It is no wonder they are having difficulty in keeping them operational; there is no compatibility. I think that we may need to take a short ride on each of their existing railroads, to see if they too are as diverse." Father enlisted the services of Jose for the next day. He too looked forward to riding the big trains.

The next morning Father called the front desk, and advised them that we would be indisposed until 1:00 p m. Jose joined us at breakfast. He had developed a schedule that would allow us to ride a short distance on four railroads. Right after breakfast, we began the morning's activity.

My Father was shaking his head when we said adios to Jose. Sitting at an outside café Father just sat and thought about what we had seen. When he asked me for an observation, I said,

"All of the rolling stock and engines are in a poor state of repair."

He nodded and said, "I think that I had better send a wire."

He took out some paper and began to write. He wadded the paper up and began again. When, he did it again. I looked a question.

He looked at me for a minute, then, said,

"It has to be in code. Motioning for me to come to his side, then he said,

"It is a code, which we agreed to use, in case it was necessary for something urgent. The reader is to use only every third word in the body of the telegram. Here, perhaps you can help in this."

We struggled to write our real message using every third word. First he wrote what he wanted to say, then we filled in other words to make it sound like it said something else. It took some time, but finally it was completed. It read:

ATCHISON, TOPEKA, & SANTA FE RAILROAD
KANSAS CITY, MISSOURI USA
FOR: CEO

*AS YOU **NOW** ARE TO **KNOW,** I UNDERSTAND **THEIR** VERY DETAILED **RAILROAD** PLAN.*

*IN SUM, **DOE'S** SEEM TO **NOT** CONSIDER A **LOOK** AT THE **GOOD** TERRAIN FEATURES.*

*PLAN IS **ALSO** FOR MANY **STOPS.** EXPECT THE **WORST** IS PAST.*

W. MARKANIS

As we entered the hotel lobby, Father gave the Desk Clerk the paper, and said,

"Please send that right away. Charge it to my room."

Since the Desk Clerk did not have a message for us, Father said,

"Well, Luke, we may be at loose ends this afternoon. What do you think of a stroll, along the beach and a look at the docks?"

Wow, I had never seen such white sand and skimpy swimsuits. There was something almost hypnotizing, about the regular waves that softly caressed the beach.

Sunbathing was evidently a major thing, because the beaches were well populated. An almost army of fellows hawking umbrellas, towels and sun cream constantly walked the beaches.

I believe that I too could become what they calling a Beach Bum. Just watching the surf and the skimpy clad bathers could develop a rush. I decided that I would need to take a present back for Mrs. Scott, and asked Father what he would recommend. It needed to be small, so it could survive another sea voyage followed by a railroad trip from the dock to St. Louis. I finally settled on a small hand made doll, dressed in a South America costume. I hoped that she would like it.

Father was of the opinion that it would be the thought that counted, and we had it packaged for the return trip.

CHAPTER 27
TERSE MOMENTS

At the port facility, there was a tour ship anchored in the harbor and shuttlecraft boats were disembarking laughing passengers. We could hear them talking about a plan for a big party that night. Everyone was talking about what costume they were going to wear.

Then we saw a man in a naval type uniform, with several gold stripes on his sleeves. Father struck up a conversation with the Captain of the ship. He began a discussion on why his ship could not be brought into the dock. I threw rocks into the water and watched a small fishing boat unload some tourists.

It was getting near sundown, so we began our return to the hotel. As we entered the lobby, the Desk Clerk motioned to us. From our key box, he gave my Father a telegram, which he folded and put in his pocket.

It read:

    W. MARKANIS
    RIO DE JANEIRO
    HOTEL MINAS GERAIS

    I DID **GET** *YOUR WIRE.* **OUT** *LINE RAILS* **QUICK.**

    ATCHISON,   TOPEKA,   &   SANTA   FE
    RAILROAD
    CEO

In our room Father read the telegram, and quickly reread it. Then read it very slow. Then, he handed it to me.

Looking rather sternly at me, he motioned to the balcony. Then he asked,

"Do you have anything you can not walk away from?

I looked around the room. Shook my head 'no', only the doll for Mrs. Scott, and asked,

"Are we going to leave now?" He nodded, and said,

"No more talking; we are going out for dinner. I am sorry, but we will have to leave Mrs. Scott's doll here."

It was getting dark as we walked back toward the beach, to a restaurant we had seen earlier. It was very busy, as many of the tourists from the cruise ship were having a big party.

We had hardly sat down when Father said,

"I will be right back," and headed for the toilet. I began scanning the menu, but could not read it. A waiter came by and I asked him to translate the menu for me. He had stepped about half the way through the listed dishes, when, from across the large room I saw Father waving at me. To the waiter, I said,

"That is enough, I will order when my Father returns." The waiter bowed, and went away.

I got up, stretched, and headed for the toilet. It was down a long hall. About halfway down the hall, Father turned right, and we went through a door that opened right onto the beach. Almost running, I followed Father to a small boat that had nosed into the beach. We climbed into the boat, and Father lay down in its' floor, and motioned for me to do the same.

Someone was working the oars, and slowly we headed out into the bay. It seemed like it took a long time until we bumped a set of stairs. Father grabbed me under my armpits, lifted and set me on the bottom rung, and motioned me to go up. He followed right behind me. It was a long climb up to the main deck.

At the top of the stairs, I could see that we were on the cruise ship. A steward (I discovered later, that is what they are called) led us through a maze of decks, aisles, and cabins, until he stopped at one. We were all out of breath, as the Steward took decks and halls that would be empty. He unlocked the inside cabin's door, handed Father the key, and we went in. Father locked the door.

We sat in the dark for what seemed like an hour, when we heard a faint rap on the door. Father, arose, went to the cabin door, and looked through the vent louvers on the door. Then he unlocked the door, and let a steward push a cart into the cabin. The door clicked shut as the steward departed.

By golly, I was really getting all keyed-up, waiting for I knew not what. Father turned the cabin lights on, and raised the lid that revealed some type of a fowl surrounded by vegetables. As in most secretive situations, I had to relieve my self, now that I could see the toilet. All of a sudden, I was famished.

Father smiled and said,

"Sorry about the sneaky business, but from the message in that wire I decided not to take a chance. I hope the authorities ashore will surmise that we had a crisis in our family, and had to make an urgent departure."

"The Captain was good enough to understand our situation, and we will be departing as soon as all of the tourists have returned on board. We should be-.... And then, we heard a very loud screech, and the ship moved slightly. Father laughed and continued,

"I was about to say, that the ship should be weighing anchor, and departing very soon."

Father and I attacked that bird; we made short work of it. During the meal, Father said that we would have to purchase some clothes tomorrow, by then we will be out of their territorial waters.

I asked,

"Where are we going?"

"The ship is scheduled to stop in Havana Cuba, then, go on to Miami, Florida. It will take about a week to make the trip."

With my stomach relieved of its' emptiness, I laid on one of the small beds to rest a minute. That is last I remembered.

When I awoke, it took me some time to remember where I was. I went into the smallest shower in the world, and washed all over the best I could. I was drying off, when Father came into the cabin. Looking at me he laughed, and said,

"You do not look much like a desperate under-world figure."

"What?"

Father, still laughing, said,

"That is what they called us in the cablegram the ship received this morning."

"Tell me what has happened."

Father said, "I bought you some underwear and clothes. Why don't you get dressed, and we will talk over breakfast."

Father supposed that the South American railroad Big-shot thinks that we departed with copies of their planned railroad. Thinking that we would use that knowledge to sabotage their plans, they declared us criminals.

"But," I said, "We did not do any of that."

Father frowned and said,

"Luke, few countries have a law system such as the US. Down here, the law is often bent to serve the purposes of the ruler, whether he be elected or has risen to power like a dictator."

There were few children on that big ship, and the ones on board all seemed to have a personal Nanny, that always restricted their movements. Nevertheless, I was able to last the trip. I had to; it was Father's first vacation.

The very next evening when I went to dinner at our table sitting there with Father was a strikingly beautiful woman. I got a lump in my throat, and stories of "Ship-borne Romances" came to mind. My heart took a turn, and visions of my Father and another woman bombarded my brain.

Not to interrupt anything, I eased around the dining room, to a point where Father would see me. I knew that he would wave me to him, unless he wanted me to stay away. He saw me, and stood and waved for me to come to their table. He introduced me to a Beverly Ence, a person that he had known in school. I suppose I had always known, and just did not want to think about it, but Father was still young enough to remarry. Just as I was coming to grips with this lovely lady possibly being my new mother, a very tall man approached our table.

Father introduced me to him, and said that he and Beverly were on their honeymoon. Whew! I cannot remember the rest of the conversations of that evening; my mind was focused on the possible prospects of a new mother. I wondered why I had not thought of Father remarrying before now. I looked at Father and for the first time saw that he was indeed handsome, and wondered why he had never, that I knew of, had dates with other women. Of course, the next day, I looked at the women on the ship in a new light. It was some time before that waned, and I could get back into the swing of our short vacation.

I was amazed at the various colors of the sea. I wrangled an invitation to visit the pilothouse, and as usual asked many questions. One of the first was about the color of the water. A third, or it could have been a forth officer, was assigned to answer my questions. He explained that the differences in colors were due to the depth of the water, the make up of the sea bottom, and the marine life in the Sea. It was a good education on the sea

One evening was a Casino night on the ship. I do not believe that youth are normally allowed in open gambling places, but being on the ocean in a ship, they did. I watched several of the games, none of which was of much interest, probably because I did not understand the rules. By, and as far as I could see, the ship was getting most of the money.

Father, to my surprise sat in a poker game. Once he had said something like "In a card game it is as much as man against man, as it is man against the odds."

I watched to see if I could tell if that was true. It was a draw poker game, with six men and a dealer around a table covered with green cloth, much like a billiard's table. Right away, I noticed a couple of the players were in every hand, and they lost quickly, and retired for the night. However, other passengers took their seats. I noted that Father had one of the largest stacks of chips.

The next morning at breakfast, I asked about the poker game. Father said,

"It went about like all such poker games. There were winners and losers. It was entertaining, and interesting to observe how some people play poker."

I asked, "Did you win?"

He smiled and said,

"I always win, but the key is to win small. Then you are never remembered as a card shark, or a sucker."

Havana cigars, sugar cane and warm temperatures, aptly describe Cuba. The head of the government was said to be almost a dictator. Contrary to what I expected, there were several large, modern casinos, and many Americans were there to help keep it green with dollars.

Sunbathing also was a favorite, but I was not into that, all I could think of was getting back to the good ole USA. We had already departed Cuba when a cablegram came with another assignment for Father.

CHAPTER 28
CONGRATULATIONS

After a long train ride back to Kansas City, Father was expecting almost anything. He said to me,

"It just depends on how they feel about what we did in South America." Henry met us at the Kansas City Depot with a carriage that took us to the Brown hotel. As we traversed the streets, he said,

"Well Bill, you are the hero again."

"How so?"

"Shortly after you sailed for South America, the US State Department received a message from our Ambassador down there, saying that the political situation was deteriorating fast. It seems the Big-shot was gathering all funds possible he could before launching a coup. Our boss was for recalling you right away, but the State Department asked that they let you proceed. Primarily, this was to see if our Ambassador there had been correct in his' assessment. It seems that they know you, and had every confidence that you could get out quick, if necessary."

"I suppose I should be pleased with their confidence in me, but with Luke on board, I would probably not have taken the risk."

Henry replied,

"Believe it or not, they asked me how I felt about Luke being with you, and I said that Luke would be a help, not a hindrances."

Father chuckled, hugged me, and said,

"And, you were right Henry."

After a bit, Father asked, "What is next?   Do you know?"

"Naw, but, there is something big brewing. It hasn't surfaced yet."

"I do hope we will have time to catch our breath, before the sky falls."

Henry laughed, and said,

"We are all invited to another one of those special dinners tonight at 7 p m."

I must admit that I had learned much in the last four or five years, having been involved in some exciting adventures. However, I wanted to stay in one spot for a while. I was now fifteen years old (well, almost) and, I wanted to go to school in one place for a while. Being realistic, though, I expected the worst.

That evening, as we were getting ready for the dinner date, the telephone rang. Father answered it, and I heard him say,

"Yes this is Bill."

"Oh, Hello Mrs. Scott, it is good to hear your voice."

"Yes, we had some fun in South America."

He was quiet for a spell, then,

"I really do not think you want to do that. How about your own grandchildren?"

"Mrs. Scott, you have been so good to Luke and me but we are not really your blood relation."

Another long pause, then,

"Well you know that we appreciate you, and I want you to know, that Luke thinks of you as his grandmother. Like wise, I, feel about you as if you were my mother."

"Luke and I will be grateful for your consideration. Yes. Good by."

Father hung-up the telephone, and just stood there looking at the wall. I did not feel that I should interrupt his' thinking, but my mind was gearing-up for the worst.

Finally, he turned around, looking at me, he said,

"That was Mrs. Scott."

I nodded.

"She says that she is going to put us in her Will."

I asked, "What does that mean?"

Father said, "When Mrs. Scott dies, we will receive something from her estate."

I asked, "What."

Father smiled and said, "She did not say." Then,

"Hey we are going to be late for the dinner."

Mister railroad and his wife were already at the table, and Henry joined us as we came into the dining room. First, they had to hear from my Father about our South American trip. Father quickly went through the day-by-day events, and then related some of his feelings about the future possibility of doing business there.

I was asked a few relevant questions, and responded. Then Mr. Railroad began,

"I hope that you recognize how helpful your little visit to South America has been. If you had not verified the questionable design of their planed railroad, and verified the political situation there, we, as well as the US Government, would have lost a great deal of money. But, that is the past, and it is time to move on."

"Bill I have another assignment for you and Luke." My mind said, Zoowie-me too?

CHAPTER 29
INCOGNITO

Continuing, he said, "We are beginning to feel that some of our employees that operate near the western ends of our rail lines are not performing well. It could be bad management, someone lining their pockets, or our own railroad system not being as efficient as it could be."

"I want you to travel incognito throughout the western lines and see if you can identify what is wrong. All of the other railroad lines are backing this effort."

I have enlisted a make-up artist to change your and Luke's appearances, and you are to travel as a hardware salesman; a drummer."

All were silent. More silence.

Father turned and looked at me. Stared, at me! I became uncomfortable. Then he, said,

"I don't know, I have never tried to put on an act before."

Mr. Railroad, said,

"That is just the point; you will not have to act. You will actually be a hardware salesperson. It is all arranged with a large local Kansas City firm. I had better also mention that they too would like your comments relative to their operations. In fact, your reporting will be to the hardware company, and all of your communications will then be delivered to me. I believe that will reduce any suspicions."

After a rather lengthy pause, my Father said,

"I am not a grease paint type, so the disguise for Luke and I would have to be very simple. In addition, I need to brush-up on my telegraphy, and I want Luke to become proficient in it too. It is amazing what one can discover by just standing near a telegrapher."

"We can arrange that. I hope that you will not be upset, but I have already had a fellow here in town look you over, and he thinks that growing a mustache, changing the color of your hair, and the type of clothes you wear, will do the trick. The one area that is not so easy to disguise is your voice, however, I feel certain that you two can do the job."

Father, turned and looked at me, I just nodded. Then he smiled and said,

"Let's order dinner."

The next few weeks were full of new things to learn, and most important to develop new characters. After our first session with the make-up fellow, I could see how we could be changed to represent someone else.

Telegraphy was a bit of a challenge, but I picked it up quickly. Father was a great help in learning how to recognize the autograph of a sender. Yes, each telegrapher has their own unique way of using the key, and if you listen close, you can detect their signature.

Father was deep into the hardware business, learning how to sell, and submit orders. I was allowed to hang around the corporate telegraphers, and listen.

So, it was that Mr. Charles Fink and son Keke, (Father and me) packed a new type of wardrobe, into old, well traveled, suit cases, and again departed Kansas City for the west. Our first destination was to be Dodge City, Kansas.

Upon arrival, we checked in at a hotel and tried our acting skills on that fair city. Quickly we discovered that if we spoke little, we would not seem out of place. The next morning Father called on a hardware store (it had been alerted to the fact that a new Drummer had been assigned to this area). I stayed on his coat tails for a while, but became bored when mountains of nails, windmills, and such were being discussed.

Outside on the store porch, I was challenged by a large teen, who I believed was the bully of the young boys of Dodge City. I had been forewarned that this would happen, and was ready. Father had said,

"You will probably be challenged, and the only way is to meet it head on. Get in the first punch; they will not be expecting it."

As I stood on the porch this fellow walked up and bumped me with his shoulder. I turned and said,

"Excuse me." The fellow looked at me like I was crazy, then he said,

"I can whip you."

Without any preamble, I hauled of and let him have my right to his jaw and eye. Backing up, he rubbed his jaw, and came away with blood on his hand. A strange change came across his face. Then, he bowed his head and came in wind milling his fists. I stepped aside, stuck out my leg, and tripped him. Bang, he fell into a porch post, spun around, trying to get his legs under himself. However, one foot came down off the porch, and he fell flat on his face in the dirt. He then retreated, going around behind the store.

I looked up to see that Father was standing there on the porch with the proprietor of the hardware store. Father turned to him and said,

"Boys will be boys," and smiled."

Later, in our hotel room, Father said that this Dodge City store seemed to be well run. However, he had recommended some additional items, and told the storekeeper that he would return the next day. Then he asked me to relate how the fight had started and what had happened. I went through every detail I could remember.

Father said, "I do not believe he will be back. I saw the makings of a black eye as he rounded the store."

The hardware store owner had recommended a diner down the street. "Nothing fancy," he had said, "but it is good clean well cooked basics." He was right, it was good food, nothing fancy like in Kansas City, but wholesome.

After dinner, we walked to the railroad Depot, where Father spoke with the telegrapher. He told him that he had in mind to send in this hardware orders by wire. The fellow then began a long discussion of how great the telegraph was, how fast it operated and on, and on. While he was reviewing more than we wanted to know, we were listening to the telegraph traffic, as it cricket, clicked away. There was nothing interesting on the wire so we soon went back to the hotel.

The next morning Father would not allow me to go downstairs, until he checked my disguise, then I had to check his. At the hardware store, I heard the owner say,

"I got to thinking about something you said yesterday. Do you remember, you said,

"You cannot sell an item unless you have it in stock." Before Father could respond, he said,

"Yes, I know I could order things, but having them on hand, a sale is more likely."

I wandered out side. Standing on the porch, I watched two of the bow-leggedist cowboys I have ever seen ride up, tie their horses to the hitching rail, and ramble into the store. They ignored me, which suited me fine. From inside, I could hear a discussion of a new Winchester.

I went inside and listened. One of the cowboys was interested in a new rifle, and they were debating the strengths of it and other rifles. I almost spoke up, but Father sensed that, and shook his head. That afternoon we went back to our room, and Father wrote out the order for the store.

He looked at me and said,

"You were about to say something down in the hardware store, right?" I nodded. "I know that you do not want another lecture on our place in this effort, but Luke, you have to think before you speak." I nodded.

After the late train departed, we again went down to the telegrapher at the Depot. He recognized Father, and they spoke for a few minutes, then Father said,

"I am going to try something, and I need your assistance. That fellow looked a question.

Father continued,

"I want to send my order for hardware using the telegraph. I hope that will speed the delivery, and will, in turn, improve store business." The fellow was beginning to get the drift.

"I have written out my order, in sort of a code so that competitors will not know what I am ordering. Can you do that?"

He stumbled a little but said, "Well, mostly the full text has to be sent, so that if a word is miss spelled, or not heard, the message will at least be readable."

My Father said,

"I understand, but if it is sent twice, the possibility of a message getting messed-up, will be a minimized."

He thought on that, then said,

"Yes, that would work. Do you want to try it?"

My Father handed him the written order, and watched as it was sent. Before, he could begin to send it a second time, someone down the line came on and asked,

"What is this trash?

The telegrapher, then explained what he was sending, and why it may not make sense, and therefore he would be repeating the message, to make sure that it was received correctly.

So, Father had established a way to communicate information and orders, and yet keep them private. Later, we laughed and wondered how many telegraphers would sit up all night trying to decode the hardware order?

CHAPTER 30
CATCHING CROOKS

There will be no excitement on this assignment; at least, that is what I thought. As we began to visit the rail ends, Father began to notice that some stations that were normally busy shipping cattle, were having difficulties. Father asked me to wander around the railroad depot and see if I could discover what the problem was.

After two days of that, with out making any headway, I decided to visit the cattle herds that were being held on the surrounding prairies. My clothing was that of what they called a 'city slicker' and the drovers seemed to ignore me. In just a few minutes, I heard one drover say,

"I think something is dead wrong with the railroad that can't get railcars for our herd."

Strolling back to town, I noted that there were no cattle cars on the sidings. I was to meet Father at lunch in a local diner (they served food there but it lacked someone who could cook). Father came late, so we had the place almost to ourselves. I gave him a summary of what I had heard and seen.

A deep frown came on his face. After several minutes he said,

"Luke, go to the Depot and listen to the telegraph traffic, and see of you can determine what is happening." I played the inquisitive kid that afternoon, making polite conversation mixed with a bit of gee-whiz with the telegrapher.

Soon he ignored me and I just looked and listened. Everything seemed normal, until a cowboy came in and offered $10 a car to get empty cattle cars on the siding. Some money was exchanged, but I could not see how much.

That evening, I told Father what had happened. Not very often have I seen him mad, but this was the worst ever. Stepping out on the diner's porch, we could see an engine backing cattle cars onto the siding. With me in tow, he went to the livery and rented a buggy. As we drove out of town, we could hear a herd of cattle bawling; they were being brought in for shipping. We sat and watched the cattle cars being loaded,

Father said,

"When you see the cowboy that was at the telegrapher when the deal was made, point him out to me."

Loading cattle, especially wild cattle, into cattle cars is not an easy thing to do. It took all of their herders, plus some local boys to get them in to the cars. Then, once a string of cars was loaded, the engine had to reposition empty cars to align with the loading chutes.

Finally, I saw the cowboy. He must have been the owner or his' representative, because it was obvious that he was in charge. Pointing him out, Father drove over to him and got down from the buggy. The cowboy saw him and rode over to see what was going on. Father introduced himself as a railroad representative, and asked if he had a few minutes.

He said that he was busy, but would sure like to meet him later. Father suggested they meet in our hotel room, and asked that he keep the meeting private, requesting that he come to our room via the rear stairs. That cowboy looked long and hard at my Father, then, asked,

"Are you a lawman?"

"No, but on the railroad, I can be even more effective than a lawman."

Another long looking at Father, and he said,

"Good. I will see you later."

It was almost ten o'clock before we heard spurs jingling as he came down the hall. A knock on the door, and Father let the cowboy into our room. The three of us sat at a table, and my Father took out a pad of paper, and asked,

"Can you give me your name and who you represent?

He hesitated, until Father said,

"If you desire I will give you this pad when we complete our discussion."

Father had a way with people, a way that seemed immediately to instill a great trust in him.

The Cowboy said,

"My name is Keith McCoy, I am the ramrod for the Double C (Brand C-C) ranch in Texas. I just drove about a thousand head of cattle up the trail, and I assume that you saw them being loaded onto the train this evening."

Father nodded, then, said,

"This is my son Luke he is young, but very good at investigations. Perhaps you noticed him at your camp fire last evening."

He shook his head no, and Father said,

"I assure you that he was there. I am going to have him tell you what he saw and heard today."

I related my visits to the telegraph office, the cattle herd, and saw the money change hands at the telegrapher's window.

CHAPTER 31
COERCION

Father said, "I believe that someone employed by the railroad is skimming money by requiring payment for services that are normally provided as part of the normal railroad's shipping fee. In short, I believe that you were coerced to pay to have cattle cars brought here for shipping your herd of cattle. Am I on the right track?"

He nodded.

Father continued, "Such activity could be as simple as a telegrapher delaying routing, or as serious as a conspiracy including the Engineers and Conductors. I have no authority to cause you to do anything, however I can promise you that if you will assist us, we will stop these improper actions.

Keith asked. "How can I help?

"We need to know just how deep in the railroad this problem goes. When is your train leaving?"

"At midnight!"

"So we have about an hour to get our act together. I want you to take Luke with you on the cattle train, he will help wherever needed, but he really understands the telegraph. If possible, I want him to listen to telegraph traffic; if possible at each and every stop. I assume that the cattle are going to Kansas City?"

He nodded.

"Before you get on the train, I want you to introduce me to a couple of your hands. I want them to ride south with me, and help determine who, when and how they are approached by this conspiracy. This may require that we visit other cattle shipping terminals. For their services, I will pay them five dollars a day. I do not need to tell you that I will need the best of your crew."

Keith was a man of action, and said, "I know just the fellows that you will need."

"One more thing, we can not be sending letters or telegrams that will alert those involved. I suggest that you wire your boss that all went well, and the hands are taking a holiday, or something like that."

Turning to me, he said, "When you get to Kansas City, call the Boss." I nodded.

Quickly I threw my clothes in my bag, and started for the train. I knew that I would be challenged, if I attempted to board the caboose without Keith, so I stood in the shadows waiting for him.

I felt some excitement, and wondered where all of this would lead. From Father's tone of voice, I could tell that he was afraid of the worst. At a few minutes to midnight, Keith came walking up and pushed me onto the caboose ahead of him. I had changed to range clothing, but kept my dyed hair and eyebrows.

The Conductor came by and shot me a stare, but Keith said,

"He is with us." That seemed to be ok, but the other cowboy, was some startled, until he noted Keith's frown. At just a few minutes after midnight the train began to move, slowly at first, but soon it hit its' stride and must have been zipping along at near 20mph.

I stretched out on one of the bunks and immediately went to sleep. Sometime in the night, I was rousted out to go help get some of the cattle to their feet. It was dark, cool and that train was weaving back and forth.

We had to climb up on the top of each car, open a hatch to view the situation, and if any of the cattle were down, climb down into the car and get them up. By mid morning I was wore out. Frequently having to poke cattle to their feet, stopping for fuel and water, and trying to listen to telegraph messages, at each station had exhausted me.

I did hear some suspicious telegraphs that sounded like some sort of code, but nothing I could really say was criminal intent. I tried to watch the conductor, but he too was awake and checked with the telegrapher at every stop. Yet, there were several odd sounding telegrams that were directed to conductors, but they too could have been normal traffic messages. I had an Idea.

At the next stop I sent a telegram to Henry. I knew he would be somewhere on the railroad system, It said:

```
HENRY LONG
SANTA FE RAILROAD

  ON THE WAY TO KC.

  HOPE TO SEE YOU THERE.

  WOULD  LIKE  TO  REVIEW  TODAY'S
  TRAFFIC.

YOUR FRIEND, LUKE
```

I hoped that someone would read this that would know that I was talking about the telegraph traffic.

It was just getting dark the next day when we arrived at the Cattle Yards of Kansas City. Keith and his hands were getting ready to unload the cattle, but there seemed to be a snag. Keith was approached by the Station Master, and was told that there was a train ahead of ours. Keith looked up at the ceiling, like he could not believe it. He looked at me and I nodded yes.

He got off the train, and had a quick talk with the Conductor, and almost immediately, our train pulled up to unloading chutes and, the unloading began. As we were finishing, I looked up and saw Henry standing a ways off. I nodded, no, and he nodded, an acknowledgement.

Keith paid his two hands that had rode the train with us, and told them they would have to get back to Texas on their own. After the paperwork was completed, I obtained my and Keith's bags from the train. Then Keith and I began to walk toward the street that serviced the Stock Yards. Hailing a carriage, one pulled right in front of us, loading our bags, we climbed in, and I told the driver "Up-town."

On the way, I told the carriage driver to take us to the Brown Hotel. Keith asked,

"Isn't that a bit expensive?" I smiled.

Henry was standing on the walk in front of the hotel. He gave me a hug, and shook Keith's hand, and said, "I called ahead and made room reservations."

In my room, I told Henry what was suspected and what Father was doing, and how Keith had been quick to help. Henry said,

"I have a group of corporate telegraphers' gathering as much of yesterday's traffic as possible. I guess that you two are pretty well exhausted. I suggest that a nap may be in order, and Mr. Big wants to have a dinner meeting at seven."

I looked at Keith and he smiled back. Then I said,

"Henry we had probably better meet in a private room to discuss these developments. A slip of the tongue could cause every thing to go quiet.

Henry said, I see what you mean. I will leave a call for you for six," and he left.

Keith went to his room, and I crashed in a very nice bed.

A telephone ringing woke me up. I sat there dumfounded for a few seconds, before I remembered where I was. I picked up the phone and said, OK, I am awake.

Oh! That bath felt good. I got dressed and was about to go see if Keith was up, when someone knocked on the door. When I opened the door, Henry was standing there with a couple of Bellhops, and a large table and folding chairs. I ushered them in, watched them setup the table and chairs. As they were leaving, Keith came in.

Keith said, "I almost could not sleep in that fancy room. I am used to sleeping under the chuck wagon."

We had a laugh over that remark.

Mr. Big came rumbling in, he barely fit through the door, and I introduced Keith. After they had shook hands he looked down at his hand, and said,

"I know that you fellows won't believe this, but my hand was like yours at one time; Almost one big callus." Everyone laughed.

Gathering around the table, I gave a quick overview of what had happened, and my Father's Suspicions. Keith related how he had been politely coursed out of ten dollars for each cattle car and practically held-up at the stockyards.

Chapter 32
How to Stop Coercion

Mr. Big really got upset, red in the face and said some rather nasty words. Then he apologized. Then Henry detailed what he had done after receiving my telegram.

Then he said,

"Any minute now, I am expecting that someone will bring me a summary of what they have discovered."

Mr. Big sat there in stony silence; like we were not even there. After a few minutes, he looked around the room at each of us and said,

"I want you to know that I, and the company greatly appreciate what you have done to fret out some of our dirty laundry. You will be rewarded!

Now, let's get our heads together and see if we can devise a way to identify those who are involved?"

We all looked at each other, but no one spoke. He looked directly at me and said,

"Luke, do you have any ideas?"

"It seems that they are using the telegraph system to control what they are dong." Everyone nodded.

"I wonder if there is a way to have every telegrapher, sign every telegram he sends.

Henry, said, "I see, if we knew who was personally involved, action could be taken."

I nodded.

Mr. Big said, "Yes, but that would require every telegram to contain two or more words, which could possibly cause a traffic jam."

Keith said, "Well, it is most difficult to work it from the drover's aspect, because he is embarrassed, thinking it was his fault that he was not on time, and thus he is reluctant to even discuss it."

Mr. Big asked, "How would we determine who sent the wire; the telegraphers or the Conductors?

I said, "We need some 'carrot on a stick', to entice those involved to become recognizable through the telegraph system."

A Knock on the door interrupted our discussions. It was the fellow working for Henry. He was seated at the table and Henry said,

"Everyone here is involved in this analysis, so you can speak freely."

He began by saying, "We have completed our first read through of yesterday's traffic. To be honest, we detected nothing out of the ordinary. However, when Henry asked that we correlate it with yesterday's cattle shipments some things came to the surface."

"With very little digging we saw where cattle cars seemed to be parked at odd places on side tracks. A closer look revealed that many empty cattle cars were parked close to the requested shipping points, when there was no reason why they did not go directly to the actual loading points."

All was quiet. Then Henry said, "So, if we had a central cattle car management dispatcher, he could direct their movement, and require that their arrival be transmitted to him?"

Mr. Big said, "Yes, that would work, but we would still have those slouches working in our system."

I said, "Why don't we bait the suspected culprits?"

Mr. Big asked, "How so?"

"We could put an agent at every cattle shipping point, and he could relay to Henry when a big herd was about to arrive."

"Then we could send a team to that shipping point that will monitor what is happening. I know that these agents would need to be trained, but I think that it is workable."

Mr. Big looked at Henry and asked, "What do you think?

Henry said, "I like it, but I need to sleep on it." In the mean time, we may hear from Bill. He always has good ideas."

Mr. Big, said "Good. Now lets all go to dinner."

It was a gala dinner, Mr. Big, spared no expenses.

The next morning, Henry brought me a telegram that he had received from Father.

It said,

"MAKING PROGRESS.

RETURNING TO KC.

DETAILS TO FOLLOW.

BILL

Two days later, I was in Father's arms for a big hug. Another council was set, and again it was in my and my Father's room.

Henry reviewed our last meeting and told of our preliminary plan for identifying the culprits.

Mr. Boss, said,"Bill lets hear what you have discovered."

Father told of visiting three herds, two of which had already been contacted by individuals warning the owner or drive boss, of special shipping fees.

Then he said, "More than ever I feel this is a conspiracy, one that has its roots in many levels of the railroad's operations."

Mr. Boss stared at Father for some time, and then asked, "Is it only with cattle shipping?"

"I think so."

"What do you think of our plan to put a team out into our system to identify those involved?"

"I believe it is the only way that I can see, short of trying to infiltrate their organization."

It was getting on toward the end of the season, where number of cattle shipped was becoming less and less. So, they began to put together a plan on how to proceed. In the middle of the planning, one night, Mr. Boss brought in a member of the Pinkertons Detective Agency. His name I will not mention, as he wanted it that way.

He listened intently as each of us related our efforts to determine just how deep the conspiracy was. He stopped us several times to ask questions. He then asked that a map of the railroad be brought to the room. While we were waiting for that item, he plied us all with deep questions, questions that we had not thought of.

After reviewing the map and asking a few more questions, he said, "Infiltration is the only way we can determine who and to what level it exists."

Mr. Boss said, "I know that you have your own operatives, but I want you to know that the men in this room are available if needed."

Then the Pinkerton fellow looked at me, and asked "Luke included?"

Everyone looked at me, but Father said, "Only, if there is no other way." He nodded.

The Pinkerton agent then turned to Mr. Boss and said, "None, I mean no one inside your company is to know that anything is amiss. I do not care if you think they are the salt of the earth, they are not to know that the Pinkertons are involved. Do you understand?"

He thought about that for a few minutes, and said, "I understand. As of today, only the men you see in this room know of this problem."

Turning, the Pinkerton Agent said, "I could use Keith, because he is not a known railroad employee, if you can spare him?"

We all laughed, because he was the only one not on the railroad payroll.

We were asked, to make our selves available for the next week, to answer any questions that may arise. There were many!

That next week we had a variety of men and boys come to our room to ask questions. Some came up the fire escape, and one even came in a Bellhop uniform. A few wore disguises, and I do not think that we would know them later, even if we met them on the street.

However, all of these fellows had one very prominent feature; they were very smart. They asked no dumb questions, nor did they ask any "What do you think" questions. By the end of the week, Keith disappeared; where he went, or who was paying his salary, was also unknown.

My Father told me about the fellow Alan Pinkerton, who had started this detective agency. I asked, "Do you think he was one of the men we talked to?"

My Father said, "No, he died some time ago."

That week my Father had received a telegram from his' lawyer in New York. It requested his presence, as some serious decisions need to be resolved. When he broke the news that he was probably going to have to go to New York, I winced.

He made several telephone calls to New York, but finally he decided that he was going to have to go. I was not excited about going east again, and voiced my position frequently. Finally, Father said,

"Luke, I need to find a place you can stay for maybe a whole year."

Then, Father, was asked to go to Wichita, Kansas on an assignment. I was not sure what was in progress, but I do know everyone thought it was serious. Because Wichita was no longer a cattle-shipping railhead, I knew it was not in support of the Pinkerton effort.

CHAPTER 33
WICHITA

The next week we departed for Wichita, and the windy west. Wichita was a bustling town, one that was growing fast, and was a pioneer jumping off place for the Oklahoma Territory Land Rush.

As we rode the railroad, south, Father told me of the situation we would be working on. In Washington D. C., a rival railroad was trying to obtain a license to run a railroad from Wichita south into Oklahoma, Territory. Their representative in Washington D.C. had made a case for the need to have more railroad competition. However, the Santa Fe Railroad, had tracks north from Wichita into Kansas City, and could provide guaranteed freight tonnage for the proposed line that would go into Oklahoma.

Father was to try to discover, who, was supporting this pending license. He thought that I might nose around boys my age and see if I could hear of anything interesting.

To get started, Father enrolled me in school. The first day I went to school, when the teacher called the roll, he read my name as "Luke Mark." How it became truncated, I will probably never know. However, I became Luke Mark. My Father got a big laugh out of it, because the school had made me incognito. Immediately Father became "Bill Mark!"

My first day of school I met a very cute girl, by the name of Katie. She was something special, but my experience with women/girls was minimal. However, she was easy to talk to and we shared some homework assignments. I think we just enjoyed each other's company. Father must have heard something of our joint efforts, because he asked me to describe Katie.

That was difficult, because I had never really looked at her that way. However, I did, and then relayed my appraisal to my Father.

He smiled!

We had been there over a week when we got our first break in the railroad question. During a recess, where the boys were talking about their parents, one fellow said that he could not talk about his Fathers work. The boy's name was Don Wight. When I passed that on to Father, he smiled and said,

"That was one of the fellows I have suspicions of. At least it will give me a place to start."

A few days later, Father was invited to join a weekly poker game, in which Mr. Wight often attended. Father described Mr. Wight as an aggressive poker player, and one who loved to close people out by raising the pot to its limit. He seemed to want to present a picture of "Better than Thou."

Two weeks went by, then, the cards came Father's way. Father, then pressed Mr. Wight hard, to the point where he seemed to loose his cool. In a classic gambling dare, Mr. Wright jumped in to a large pot. In sum, Father cleaned him out.

The next day Mr. Wight sought out Father, trying to interest him in a new railroad that was just being organized. He offered Father the opportunity to invest; a chance to buy a block of stock in an emerging railroad company. However, he could not disclose the name of the company. As always, Father cautiously hinted that he had just recently come into a bit of money. Mr. Wight responded with a deal where he offered an opportunity to purchase a block of stock for ten thousand dollars.

That night Father and I sat up late writing a telegram to Mr. Boss, that said,

> MR. BOSS
> KANSAS CITY, MISSOURI
>
> *HAVE DISCOVERED OPPORTUNITY TO PURCHASE A BLOCK OF STOCK IN NEW DEVELOPING RAILROAD INTO OKLAHOMA TERRITORY.*
>
> *WILL REQUIRE TEN THOUSAND DOLLARS.*
>
> *PLEASE ADVISE*
>
> W. MARK

Father felt sure that Mr. Wight would somehow obtain a copy of this telegram, so it had to sound real. Father had told Mr. Wight that he would need a few days to make up his mind.

The next day a telegram arrived:

> W. MARK
> WICHITA, KANSAS
>
> *INTERESTING POSSIBILITY.*
>
> *NEED TO KNOW NUMBER OF SHARES TO BE ISSUED.*
>
> *FACE VALUE OF SHARES*
>
> *NAMES OF MANAGEMENT*

CONSTRUCTION TIME TABLE

BOSS

Father showed the telegram to Mr. Wight, knowing that he had probably already obtained a copy. Father said that Mr. Wight became very nervous when he read the telegram. Father's suspicions were that he had not told the other stockholders of what he was doing.

However, the other stockholders were now firing telegrams back and forth to each other. My assignment was to hang around the Depot, and listen to the telegraph traffic and take notes.

Most of the early traffic was slamming Mr. Wight for disclosing their plans; however, wanting more cash, they took the bait.

Finally, they offered Father an option to purchase a block of the company stock, for $20K. This was relayed to the Boss.

After a two day wait, the reply came.

```
W. MARK
WICHITA KANSAS

    RE: YOUR WIRE, DESIRE A LARGER
    BLOCK OF STOCK.

    NEGOTIATE WITH REPRESENTATIVE

    DETERMINE HOW MUCH STOCK CAN BE
    OBTAINED

BOSS
```

Of course, Father and I were only seeing our telegraph traffic, but could imagine what was going on in Washington D.C. If this new company had told the government that sufficient funds were on-hand to implement the requested

License, then some would wonder why they were seeking more stockholders.

It was two more days before they replied, but I was there to copy the wire, and give it to Father a day before they came to face Father.

In essence, they wanted to feel out Father and Boss, who ever that was, as to how much money could possibly be obtained. The next day, before Father wired Mr. Boss, Mr. Wight became very nervous. He would not face Father, even though he sought him out.

Then we received the following telegram.

```
W. MARK
WICHITA, KANSAS

    COMPETITIVE RAILROAD DID NOT GET
    LICENSE

    GOOD JOB
    RETURN TO KC ASAP

    NY LAWYER WIRING AND CALLING
    DAILY                     .

  BOSS
```

I did not know it, but Father had been looking into the possibility of me staying in Wichita while he went to New York. With this latest telegram closing out the license problem, Father took me to an orphanage in Wichita that could accommodate me for at least a year. The place was clean and seemed to be well run. Half of the children in the orphanage were not even orphans.

Because of the distances between town and ranches, and farms, some schoolchildren needed to live in town to attend school. So, it was decided that I would become a member of their orphanage. What sealed the decision was that, as the oldest child, I would have my own room. Small, it was; but it did give me some privacy.

I liked the local schoolteacher. He was well educated and well versed in world geography. Father told me that he had arranged to pay for my room and board, and a monthly allowance.

So, a week later I stood on the Wichita Depot platform, and waved good-by to my Father as he departed for Kansas City and New York City.

By dark I was wondering what I had gotten into? I felt alone, wondering when I would see my Father again. I hoped that I would be surprised, by a visit by Henry or Mrs. Scott, but knew that possibility was remote. Already, I felt alone!

When the News finally came, it was not what I wanted to hear!

Printed in the United States
91809LV00004B/13-162/A

9 781434 321824